Dog-Friendly
DOG TRAINING

2nd Edition

Andrea Arden

Illustrations by Tracy Dockray

BICENTENNIAL
1807
WILEY
2007
BICENTENNIAL

Wiley Publishing, Inc.

Library of Congress Cataloging-in-Publication Data:
Arden, Andrea.
  Dog-friendly dog training / Andrea Arden ; illustrations by Tracy Dockray. — 2nd ed.
     p. cm.
  Includes index.
  ISBN-13: 978-0-470-11514-5 (alk. paper)
  ISBN-10: 0-470-11514-9 (alk. paper)
  1. Dogs—Training. I. Title.
  SF431.A75 2007
  636.7'0887—dc22

                            2007007079

Printed in the United States of America

10 9 8 7 6 5 4 3 2 1

Second Edition

Book design by George J. McKeon
Cover design by Wendy Mount
Wiley Bicentennial Logo: Richard J. Pacifico
Book production by Wiley Publishing, Inc. Composition Services

For my brother George

Acknowledgments

I would like to express thanks and acknowledgment to the following:

Dr. Ian Dunbar. I am lucky to count myself among the thousands who have been influenced by Dr. Ian Dunbar. If one were to count the hours that Dr. Dunbar has spent helping people learn a better, kinder way of teaching dogs, I have no doubt they would find that he has given up years of his life in this effort. Thankfully, it has not been in vain. Because of him, dog training is fun, friendly, and full of tail wags.

Oliver and Nora, and all the dogs who are responsible for teaching me so much and who are the reason my life is what I dreamed it would be when I was a child.

Rhett, whose drive and enthusiasm for new challenges and adventures of all sorts is inspiring. He chose me as his wife, and for that I am very lucky.

Laura, who is truly the best friend.

About the Author

Andrea Arden is best known as the trainer and field host for *The Pet Department*, Fox's Emmy Award–winning show. Her appearances also include the *Today Show, 20/20, Live with Regis and Kelli, The View,* and *Dateline NBC*. She is the author of *Train Your Dog the Lazy Way, Andrea Arden's Little Book of Dog Tricks,* and *On the Road with Your Pet*. Andrea is a columnist and contributing writer for numerous magazines, including *Dog Fancy, Modern Dog,* and *The New York Dog*. She is a charter member of the Association of Pet Dog Trainers and has served on the Board of Directors of the Association of Pet Dog Trainers and Animal Haven Shelter and Sanctuary. Andrea is Director of Andrea Arden Dog Training and lives in New York City with her husband, Rhett Butler; her dogs, Nora, Moka, and Bela; and two very pretty cats named Issa and Anya.

About the Illustrator

Tracy Dockray has illustrated many books, including *Grimm's Grimmest* and *Am I Big or Little?* by Margaret Parks Bridges, and was proud to reillustrate Beverly Cleary's Ramona series, Mouse and the Motorcycle series, and Henry Huggins series, and most of her individual novels as well. Her work has also appeared in *Vogue, Travel and Leisure,* and the *New York Times.* Tracy has found *Dog-Friendly Dog Training* most helpful in training her family's new Brussels Griffon and has even found its friendly theories handy in dealing with her two small children, stepdaughter, and husband. (Don't tell them that!)

Contents

What Is Dog-Friendly Dog Training?

When it comes to the best way to train your dog, the sheer wealth and breadth of conflicting advice is often bewildering. Bookstores and pet shops sell a vast array of literally hundreds of different dog books, and each one recommends different training methods—jerk the leash, don't jerk the leash; use food, don't use food; always do this, never do that.

Worse yet, for the longest time most people have associated dog training with choke collars and leash jerks, assuming the whole process to be a chore and a drag. Wrong, wrong, wrong! An incredible rediscovery has been made in the field of dog training: Training your dog is fun! Better yet, the more fun you and your dog have while training, the faster and more effective training becomes.

Luckily for today's dogs, the popularity of reward-based training grew steadily through the 1980s and 1990s and caused a dog-friendly revolution.

Dog-friendly dog training is the best way to create the dog of your dreams.

In a nutshell, dog-friendly dog training focuses on three things:

✦ Rewarding good behaviors

✦ Preventative management

✦ Using gentle teaching methods

Focusing on Rewarding Good Behaviors

There are two objectives in training your dog: a major objective and a minor one. The major objective of friendly, intelligent pet dog training is to teach dogs *to do* things we want them to do. The secondary and minor objective is to teach dogs *not to do* things we don't want them to do.

Dog-friendly dog training zeroes in on the major objective: teaching your dog what you want and rewarding him for doing it. This is the easiest way to train your dog. After all, there aren't many things we consider "right" for pet dogs to do, so you really don't have many things to teach. On the other hand, the list of "wrong" things that pet dogs can do is endless, so trying to train by punishing your dog for each mistake would be a lengthy and unpleasant process for both of you. When you have taught your dog to reliably understand you and consistently spend his time focusing on good behaviors, he won't have the time or the inclination to behave inappropriately.

For any natural dog behavior you can come up with, there are lots of inappropriate choices and usually just a few correct ones. For example, imagine the one right spot for your dog to use as his toilet (either outside or inside on papers or pads), and imagine how nice and easy it is to take him to that spot when he needs to go (and reward him for doing so).

Teaching Right Is Easier Than Teaching Wrong

Rewarding good behavior is the central tenet of dog-friendly training. Choosing to focus on rewards rather than punishments is the most important decision you will make with respect to educating your dog. Not only is doing so more fun—for you *and* your dog!—but it is also much easier. After all, there is a rather short list of right behaviors, but an almost endless list of wrong ones.

"Right" Behaviors

- Eliminating in appropriate spot(s)
- Playing nicely with people
- Playing nicely with other dogs
- Playing with dog toys (especially food-stuffed chew toys)
- Responding to your requests (to sit, lie down, come, etc.)
- Resting calmly indoors
- Sitting to greet people
- Walking nicely on leash

"Wrong" Behaviors

- Eliminating in the house (in hundreds of different spots)
- Playing roughly with people
- Chewing on your clothes
- Chewing on your furniture
- Chewing on your plants
- Chewing on your shoes
- Chewing on your toys (CDs, books, the remote)
- Chasing the cat
- Digging in your garden
- Eating your food off the table
- Fighting with other dogs
- Guarding objects
- Jumping up on visitors
- Not responding to your requests
- Pulling on the leash
- Raiding the garbage
- Running away
- Barking for long periods
- Add your dog's annoying behaviors here:

_____

_____

You'll have a whole lot of cleaning up to do after you've allowed your dog to test out all the wrong places to go to the bathroom.

Teaching your dog the one right spot to go to the bathroom is much easier than punishing him for going in innumerable wrong places.

Now imagine the hundreds of wrong places for him to urinate and how long it would take and how unpleasant it would be to punish your dog for going in each of those spots. Likewise, picture your house after your dog has tried out all the wrong things to chew. Now imagine how much easier it would have been if you had just gotten him hooked on a chew toy or taught him the one appropriate place to eliminate.

Catch Your Dog Doing Something Right!

It may be human nature, but we tend not to notice or to ignore good behavior and instead focus most of our attention on behaviors we don't like. Try to catch your dog doing something right at least five times a day and reward him for doing it. You'll find that each day it will be easier and easier to do so, because your dog will be learning the best ways to get your attention. For example, if he walks up to you and sits in front of you, let him know how pleased you are that he chose such a polite and friendly way to say hello. The more frequently he offers the right behavior, the less time he'll have to do the wrong things.

Why else is rewarding good behavior so important? For the simple fact that once you have successfully taught your dog how you would like him to behave, he will no longer misbehave. And when he doesn't misbehave, you have no reason to be upset with him. Do yourself and your dog a favor and start teaching your dog what you want him to do the first day he comes home with you. If you already have a dog, start today!

The principle of teaching what is right makes special sense during puppyhood. Not even twenty years ago, it was impossible to enroll a dog in obedience classes until he was at least 6 months old. This would be comparable to keeping children out of school until their late teens! By 6 months of age, most of those uneducated dogs were seriously out of control and required physically rigorous and mentally demanding training methods.

Thankfully, times have changed. Puppy training is widely available, and trainers, veterinarians, shelter workers, and breeders encourage new dog owners to begin teaching their dogs on the day they take them home.

Managing Unwanted Behaviors

Dog-friendly trainers focus on getting rid of unwanted behaviors through preventative management and lack of reinforcement. For example, if you keep your dog on leash when greeting people at the front door (preventative management) and nobody reinforces jumping (lack of reinforcement), your dog won't be able to practice the behavior, won't find the behavior very rewarding, and will try to figure out what behavior *is* rewarding. He is likely to try sitting as a way to get attention, at which point you should reward him to make this the greeting behavior he chooses in the future.

If the unwanted behavior persists, try to figure out what is reinforcing it. Sometimes the behavior itself is reinforcing, as is the case with some dogs who seem to get a thrill out of barking. In this situation, focus on providing your dog with more exciting activities than barking. How about giving him every morsel of his meals from food-stuffed toys so that he is kept busy working to get his food out? Or how about using management tools such as on-leash supervision or confinement to a specific area to prevent access to the most stimulating areas of your home (doorways and windows) until he has learned that excessive barking is not appropriate?

Preventative Management

Rewarding your dog for being right is undoubtedly easier, more effective, and more fun than punishing him for being wrong. Moreover, you can speed up the process by responsibly managing your dog's life to maximize the likelihood that he will be right. This way, much of the training becomes effortless, errorless learning, and harsh correction or punishment is simply unnecessary. Simple and smart.

You should be especially concerned with management until the training takes effect. For example, until you have taught your dog to have a chew-toy habit, you should not give him unsupervised access to your home.

There are two parts to management:

+ Controlling the resources
+ Controlling the environment

Controlling the Resources

Dog resources include anything your dog likes:

+ Food (normal meals as well as special treats)
+ Praise (verbal and physical)
+ Activity-based rewards (going for a walk, playing with other dogs, getting up on the couch, riding in the car)
+ Play (games with you or just chewing a toy)

Dogs are masters at training us to do all sorts of things for them. Try to remember that you *decide* when it's dinnertime, playtime, and time to go for a walk. Better yet, use those times to reinforce desirable behaviors, such as sitting for his supper or to go for a walk.

Most owners give their dogs free access to just about everything that is valuable to the dog. In fact, dogs are often rewarded with resources when they do things the owner *doesn't* like! For example, the dog jumps around like a madman as his food is being prepared, and then the owner puts the bowl down for the dog to eat. Or the dog pulls on the leash, and the owner continues the walk. It's so much smarter to take control of these resources and use them to teach your dog to behave appropriately. In these two situations, wait to put the food down until your dog keeps all four feet on the ground, and wait to continue your walk until your dog is at your side.

Convince your dog that you hold the key to his "resource treasure chest" so that he realizes how valuable you are and how important it is to do as you ask.

Learn It to Earn It!

Your dog will benefit in endless ways if you teach him that appropriate behaviors are necessary to earn all the things he wants in life, including food, toys, attention, play with other dogs, and trips to the park. This approach is the best way to become your dog's guide through a long, happy life with you.

Controlled access to a limited commodity increases its value. It's all a matter of supply and demand. If something is easily accessible and in great supply, the demand usually isn't so great. Imagine if you had twenty million dollars. If someone asked you to do something for one dollar, chances are you would not be very motivated to do it. Consequently, make your dog's resources more valuable by controlling them. For example, pick up all your dog's toys and ask him to come, sit, or lie down before you give him one or two to play with. Each time he comes to you for petting, ask him to do something before you comply. When you serve him his dinner, ask him to do something before you put his food-stuffed toy or bowl on the floor. Better yet, every once in a while, sit down and hand-feed him some of his meal and ask him to do something for *each piece* of food.

Similarly, when walking your dog on leash, regularly stop and wait for him to look at you and to sit before you continue walking. He will quickly learn that watching you and sitting when you stop is the way to ensure that the walk will continue. Let your dog know that you have what he wants, and if he wants it, he just needs to ask politely—in this case, by sitting at your side when you stop walking.

Don't feel bad about asking your dog to do a little something in return for resources. Dogs love to have a job to do. Most pet dogs have no job, and in turn they have a very boring existence. You, however, can change all that.

A Working Dog Is a Happy Dog

No matter what your dog's size or type, he still needs a job to feel fulfilled and to achieve his full potential. Your dog's jobs can include hunting for his food from food-stuffed toys, responding to your requests, and maybe even fetching your slippers!

Controlling the Environment

By preparing your house in such a way that your dog does not have access to areas where he might make mistakes, you are essentially putting the odds in your dog's favor that he will be right. Doing so from the outset with a new puppy or dog will prevent predictable behavior problems and the potential need for punishment. This is also the best way to prevent further problems with your current dog. Of course, once your dog reliably understands the house rules, he can enjoy as much freedom indoors as you permit.

Attention, Please

A result of controlling the things your dog wants is that you will get his attention. Attention is crucial if you intend to teach him. When your dog pays attention to you (and then follows your instructions), he has an opportunity to have you unlock the door to all the things he loves.

How can this dog not misbehave? The only options he has to occupy his time are ones that will annoy his owner. Creating a dog-friendly home, one in which he has little opportunity to make mistakes, is one of the kindest things you can do for your dog.

Controlling your dog's access to areas where he might get into trouble is known in the dog-training trade as the "shut the door" notion. For example, if your dog is getting into the garbage in the kitchen, shut the kitchen door, confine your dog away from the kitchen, or get a garbage can with a lid that locks. If your dog is urinating in your bedroom, shut the bedroom door. Better yet, confine your dog to an exercise pen, a crate, or one room in the house. If you confine your dog, there are a thousand wrong things he can't do in the other rooms. This is essentially the same way we teach young children to behave at home. You wouldn't consider allowing a toddler to roam around unsupervised!

When you have time to supervise him, you can also keep your dog on leash at your side with a couple of food-stuffed toys. Doing so prevents so many problems that it would take a whole book to write them down. If you keep your dog on leash until he learns the house rules, he can't chew inappropriate things, eliminate in the wrong places, and so on. This is, of course, a temporary but necessary aspect of training. Once the dog has learned good habits, a lifetime of freedom in the home awaits.

Set Your Dog Up to Be Right

Stack the deck in your dog's favor so that he can't fail to be right. If this is done properly, he should have no alternative but to behave in the way you would like. For example, leave your dog in a crate or a protected room with three food-stuffed chew toys, and you are pretty much assured that your dog will quickly learn to enjoy chewing chew toys rather than a host of inappropriate household articles. He can't destroy your house or bark incessantly if he is engrossed in his chew toys.

Using Gentle Teaching Methods

When teaching your dog to respond on cue, he learns that the Antecedent (a cue, request, or command) followed by a specific Behavior (such as sit, down, or come) signals that a Consequence (reward) is likely to follow. These are the ABC's of teaching:

Antecedent–Behavior–Consequence

A reward (Consequence) causes the behavior to increase in frequency. For example, simply giving your dog a piece of food every time he sits quickly produces a sit-happy dog who sits frequently. The reward also reinforces the association between the request and the response, such that the dog learns that sitting when requested often produces rewards. Ultimately, the dog learns to *want* to sit on request. If you want your dog to sit frequently without even being asked (such as at street corners or when greeting people), you can reward him when he places his rear on the floor without the cue. This is an automatic sit in specific situations. This way, he'll learn that sitting, whether he's asked to or not, is a good idea.

This training sequence represents an oversimplification of learning theory—the science of dog training. But your dog is going to learn very quickly if you present the ABC's.

Some examples of the ABC's of learning are:

Antecedent	Behavior	Consequence
The dog hears you pick up the leash.	The dog comes to you.	You put the leash on your dog and take him for a walk.
The dog hears the word "sit."	The dog sits.	You give the dog a tasty treat and praise.
The dog hears the doorbell.	The dog goes to the door and sits.	You open the door.

The art of dog training, though, depends very much on the skill of predicting or causing the behavior you are trying to put on cue and increase in frequency. For example, when you ask the dog to sit, how can you predict that the dog will sit so that you can reward him for doing so?

How you go about this is the main determinant of the efficiency and effectiveness of training. Basically, three techniques are used to predict or cause specific behaviors:

1. Simply waiting for the behavior to happen on its own (capturing/shaping)

2. Luring the behavior to happen (lure/reward training)

3. Physically prompting the behavior

As a dog-friendly trainer, you will primarily use numbers 1 and 2, gentle capturing and shaping and lure/reward methods, to motivate your dog

Brain or Brawn?

Brain power is far superior to physical power when it comes to dog training (and just about everything else, as a matter of fact!). Instead of trying to master difficult, time-consuming, and largely ineffective physical methods to punish your dog for countless wrongs, why not teach your dog what you want him to do by using reward-based techniques? It is so much easier and quicker, and a darn sight more enjoyable for you *and* your dog.

Almost everybody, including children, can train with their brain, but few people can master the rigors of physical training methods, and even fewer people enjoy this approach.

to do what you want. Everyone, including children, can easily master these two quick and fun ways to train.

Physical prompting methods, on the other hand, are not appropriate for all dogs and all people. A child certainly should not be expected to physically prompt a dog to get him to obey. Even adults may be at risk if they resort to pushing and pulling some dogs. Overall, physical prompting is not as safe, easy, or effective as the other two approaches, and it's probably not as fun for you or your dog.

Why Not Use Punishment?

A consequence of a behavior can be pleasant or unpleasant. While pleasant consequences reliably increase the behavior they follow, the result of unpleasant consequences is not as predictable. Unpleasant consequences often create anxiety and confusion and sometimes increase the frequency of other unwanted behaviors. For example, punishing a dog for urinating in one spot in the house may cause the dog to be scared to eliminate in your presence, in which case he may hide from you and eliminate in multiple spots throughout the house.

The stress from punishment comes from pain, but also from the dog's confusion. Because most punishment happens after the fact, it is unlikely that the dog understands why he is in trouble, and therefore he is likely to become confused and stressed and may possibly shut down. Dogs in this state are sometimes mistakenly labeled as stubborn. In fact, the dog is opting out of the training game because he simply doesn't understand how to play the game. Imagine if you were being tutored in a new language, and each time you made a mistake your teacher rapped you on the hand or yelled at you. Chances are you would not show up for future lessons, and you obviously would not learn this new language.

Capturing

The capturing method of training is also referred to as reward training. Capturing is an extremely simple method to master, and it is the method most likely to result in a reliably trained dog who, as a wonderful side benefit, has mastered the ability to learn.

Learning to Learn

Using this method can maximize your dog's potential by encouraging him to be an active, thoughtful participant in training. This approach creates a dog whose ability to learn is greatly improved; he becomes very much a "thinking dog" who is confident and enthusiastic about playing the training game.

Using gentle, motivation-based training you will be creating a dog who is a terrific problem solver.

All you have to do is wait for the right behavior to occur spontaneously before marking the behavior (with the sound of a clicker or "yes") and then reward the dog.

For something simple such as a sit, the behavior is likely to happen quickly and is therefore easy to capture. For more complicated behaviors, such as jumping through a hoop, you shape the behavior by marking and rewarding small steps in the right direction toward the ultimate goal. For example, you might start by marking and rewarding the dog for stepping toward the hoop, which is held low to the ground. Then you might reward him for touching it with his nose, then for stepping a paw through it, and then his whole body, gradually increasing the height the hoop is held off the ground.

What Is a Marker?

A marker tells your dog *exactly* which behavior earned a reward. The marker occurs at the same exact time as the desired behavior or event, which is why some people call it an *event marker*. The marker is immediately followed by a reward.

A marker can be a word, such as "yes," but is more effective when it is a distinct and unique sound, such as the click of a clicker—a small, handheld tool that you press with your thumb. Unlike your voice, the sound of the click never varies. Also, the sound of the click is much easier for your dog to recognize than one word (such as "yes") in what is probably a stream of words you are saying to him. As such, it's easy for your dog to learn that the click means only one thing: What I did at the exact moment I heard a click is getting me a reward. This clear, sharp sound can have a dramatic impact on the clarity of your communications with your dog.

It usually takes just a few repetitions of pairing the marker with the reinforcement for your dog to associate the two. Since your dog wants to increase the likelihood of the reinforcement, he will increase (repeat) the behavior that happened when he heard the click.

Unlike lure/reward training, where both you and your dog exert relatively similar effort, capturing requires your dog to be the more active participant, to try to figure out what is expected at a certain moment in order to be reinforced. Your job is to carefully observe your dog so that you can deliver well-timed and frequent reinforcements.

Generally, at first, reward training takes more time than lure/reward training. When you start, you are waiting for the dog to behave appropriately, and it usually takes him at least a few guesses to get it right.

During reward training, your dog will make many mistakes and incorrect guesses at what you want, but each unrewarded mistake is important because it enables your dog to eliminate yet another unprofitable option. The more mistakes, the more your dog learns what is *not* rewarding. Eventually, your dog will hit upon what you want, and will soon repeat the immediately rewarded behavior many times. Dogs love playing this game.

For example, to train your dog to sit, take hold of a few pieces of his food, stand still, and wait for him to sit. He may go through a whole repertoire of behaviors, like jumping up and barking. Ignore all this and wait for the sit—he will do it eventually. When he sits, click or say "yes," offer him a piece of food, and then do it again. (You might have to take a step to get your dog to stand up.) You will find that your dog sits more and more quickly each time. Soon, your dog will develop the notion of sitting after you take a step in order to hear the click or the word "yes," which

Reward training techniques are extremely effective, which is why they are used almost exclusively for training bomb-detection dogs, search-and-rescue dogs, and top-notch obedience and agility competition dogs. These techniques produce reliable, happy dogs.

means that he gets a reward. Now you can predict when he will sit and say the word right before he does so—in this case, right as you are about to stop after taking a step.

This technique is terrific for teaching all-or-nothing behaviors like sit and down. More complicated behaviors like a retrieve or a fancy trick are shaped by rewarding the dog for successive approximations to the desired behavior—when it's not exactly what you want, but the dog is headed in the right direction.

What If My Dog Doesn't Obey?

Reward-trained dogs want to perform behaviors that they have learned result in rewards. If your dog truly understands what is expected and desires the reward, he will respond appropriately. If he doesn't, don't assume that he is being spiteful or disobedient. Instead, ask yourself, Does he really understand what I'm asking in this environment, and am I being sufficiently rewarding?

Reward training is wonderful for all types of dogs, whether they are reserved (it helps build confidence) or aggressive (it helps build a stellar relationship between dog and handler and creates a dog who has a more positive outlook). Reward training is the method of choice for active and excitable adolescent dogs. It calms dogs more quickly than any other method. You simply ignore the adolescent antics and wait for the dog to do something good. It's the quickest way to train an adolescent dog to pay attention, walk on leash calmly, and sit automatically when you stop. Dogs quickly learn that goofy antics like jumping about and barking don't make anything happen, but standing still, sitting, and lying down are like switches that turn you on and give them praise, treats, and play time.

Anybody can reward train from anywhere, even when relaxing in an armchair. Reward training is great for all types of trainers, especially children and the elderly. Reward training methods are calming. There is no need to be upbeat and exciting. Instead, you can relax and enjoy watching your dog figure things out. Moreover, since you give no commands at the beginning, no one has any idea what you are trying to do, so you can't look silly if your dog doesn't quickly do what you have in mind! Don't worry, though; in no time at all, everyone will know exactly what you are doing as they look on in amazement.

Markers and Treats Forever?

Once your dog understands a behavior on cue, there is not necessarily a need to click or offer a treat. However, you should maintain learned cues and behaviors by using a variety of reinforcements, including going for a walk, playing with another dog, and playing fetch. However, when you teach a new behavior or an "old" one in a new environment or around new distractions, you should use your marker and treats.

Lure/Reward Training

Luring is a way of getting your dog to move by holding a treat on his nose so that he follows the treat and goes into various positions when you move your hand. Lure/reward training is a hands-off method to get your dog to do what you want him to do and then reward him for doing it.

Food from the dog's normal, daily diet is perhaps the best way to lure, but special treats, tennis balls, and stuffed chew toys also work well. You can entice your dog to move his nose, which gives you control over his entire body, just by moving a small lure. By manipulating the lure, you can:

- Modify the dog's body position (sit, down, stand, roll over, spin)
- Modify the dog's direction of movement (come here, go there)
- Get him to focus on specific objects (chew toys, tennis balls, you)
- Modify natural canine behaviors (chewing, digging, barking)

Lure/reward training is an effective way to get your dog to enjoy training and the trainer. For example, ask your dog, "Do you like training with me as much as I do with you?" and then move a piece of food up and

Using lure/reward training, anyone, regardless of age or physical strength, can position any size dog.

down in front of your dog's nose. Magically, he will nod his head in agreement. Then offer the food lure as a reward for agreeing with you!

Lure/reward training has numerous beneficial side effects, but the best is that it teaches your dog to like all types of people, especially children, men, and strangers. Dogs quickly learn to enjoy the company of anyone who takes the time to ask them to come, sit, lie down, and roll over in this gentle and rewarding manner. Your dog will also learn to like hands moving around his head and body. Most important, lure/reward methods offer an easy, nonconfrontational means for children to commandeer respect from the dog and train him to be happily and willingly compliant. Obviously, children can't and shouldn't physically force a dog to do anything, but with lure/reward training, children can exert mental control.

All reward-training techniques have advantages; because of its efficiency and gentleness, lure/reward training is a good method of choice.

What If My Dog Doesn't Like Food?

If your dog is disinterested in the food lure, teach him to thoroughly enjoy food by hand-feeding him for a few days. In the meantime, interact with your dog using what he does like, such as praise, affection, balls, toys, games, and activities. For example, use your hand to lure the dog to sit and invite him onto the couch as a reward. Or use a tennis ball to lure him to come, but pet and praise him as a reward. However, because lure/reward training with food is so effective, it would be a smart prospect to train your dog to show a greater interest in it. You can pique your dog's interest in food by leaving his meals down for just five to ten minutes at each feeding so that he learns to eat promptly, and by reserving his meals for training times. This way, you are teaching your dog when he is most likely to be focused on how to achieve the task at hand so that he may earn his food.

Physical Prompting

For years, dog training was pretty much synonymous with leashes and collars. The very notion of dog training conjured up visions of a trainer snapping the dog's collar with the leash to motivate him to heel, or tugging upward on the leash and firmly pushing down on the dog's rump to place him in a sit. At first, physical prompting seems extremely efficient and effective because the dog appears to respond promptly. However, physical prompting is deceptively complicated, and it usually takes an experienced trainer to avoid negative side effects.

This method requires:

✦ Physical strength to push, pull, and jerk

✦ Absolute consistency so that your dog learns that punishments are always an option

✦ An excellent understanding of dog behavior so that you lessen the chances of getting hurt by a dog who fights back

One of the biggest flaws in some dog-training methodologies is that many trainers underestimate their own expertise. What comes so easily to them after twenty-five years of experience falls apart in the hands of a novice owner working with a novice dog.

Additional flaws to this approach include the fact that the dog may be distracted by the touch, and it overrides the other intended cues, such as verbal cues. Of equal importance is the notion of opposition reflex. One of Newton's laws of motion is "For every action, there is an equal and opposite reaction." So, if you push or pull your dog one way, chances are he will attempt to maintain his balance by pushing or pulling the other way. For example, if you try to push him to the floor, his natural reaction will be to brace his legs.

Few of us will succeed by jerking our dogs around. And if you're working with a fearful or aggressive dog, physical prompting can result in disaster. An example is jerking a dog by the leash when walking down the street. If you do this frequently enough when passing children or other dogs, the dog may learn to associate a harsh correction with them passing. This association could understandably lead to some negative feelings—or worse.

Physical prompting requires that you have the requisite strength and agility to physically position your dog.

The Four E's of Training

Capturing

EASE   Talk about easy. This is the time to relax and meditate. Make sure to take this book along so that you have something to read while you wait for your dog to offer a behavior you like. Once he does, mark the behavior with a click of your clicker or by saying "yes," and then reward him with a tiny treat. After the first five to ten correct behaviors are marked and rewarded, your dog will start to understand what you want. Now things start to move at a quicker pace, and in no time at all the dog's performance is improving in leaps and bounds before your very eyes.

EFFECTIVENESS   Capturing produces a highly reliable performance because your dog is required to work through problems on his own and therefore develops a clear understanding of the task. Over time, the reliability is enhanced, because capturing increases a dog's attentiveness by

Friendly training methods have been used for years to train dolphins, whales, and grizzly bears. After all, you can't very well put a choke collar on a whale and jerk him around a tank to get him to do want you want. If we can train these animals with friendly methods, we can certainly train our pet dogs the same way!

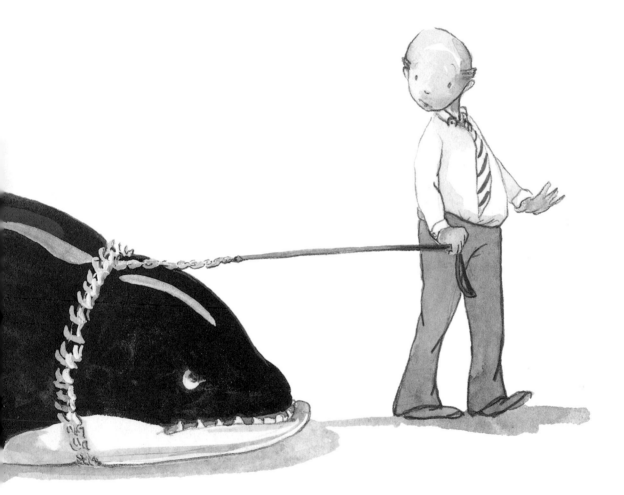

teaching him to be a great problem-solver and to be addicted to playing the training game with you. This method is ideal for all family members to work with all types of dogs, especially rambunctious and unruly ones. In fact, the more rambunctious and inattentive the dog, the better the effect. A dog of this type greatly benefits from learning to focus in order to problem-solve.

EFFICIENCY   Capturing is like getting on a roller coaster. The start of the ride may move a bit slowly, but then it takes off at a lightning pace, and before you know it, you're flying along.

ENJOYMENT   Everyone (dogs included) loves capturing. One of the most enjoyable things about this way of teaching is demonstrating it to others. Of all the techniques in dog training, this one has the highest feel-good factor, since you'll feel an amazing connection with your dog. As your dog learns to pay attention to your body language and to read every nuance and intention of your movements, you'll soon get the feeling that your dog is looking at you like you are his sun, moon, and stars!

Lure/Reward Training

EASE   This method is easy to master, and almost everybody in the family can do it. All you have to do is keep your hand steady and move the lure slowly to entice the dog to assume different positions. You can even keep your other hand in your pocket or behind your back.

EFFECTIVENESS   This is one of the most effective training techniques because the sheer speed and enthusiasm of the dog's responses make it possible to practice many responses in a single training session. It is easy to master and to progressively practice for better reliability. Just as you repeat physical exercises to build muscle, so will you need to build your dog's learning muscles. Lure/reward training is an easy way to build reliability through rapid repetition.

EFFICIENCY   The use of the lure in training is almost magical. An untrained puppy or adult dog can be lured into a sit, down, or stand—in fact, into any body position—in no time at all. Lure/reward training is *very* fast. It is a good method for a large percentage of the things you want to teach your pet dog.

ENJOYMENT   Lure/reward-trained dogs have fun, and their enthusiasm is infectious. Training a dog who is having a good time is fun! Since this method is so easy, the entire family, including supervised children, can take part in the training game.

Physical Prompting

EASE   Physical methods are difficult for many owners, especially children, to master. Many novice owners understandably become frustrated in their attempts to master apparently simple techniques, which actually require considerable precision and strength.

EFFECTIVENESS   Physical prompting techniques often give the appearance that the dog is better trained than he is. The dog may look good on leash, but this is often a result of being shut down. He may act as if he has never been trained when released. In fact, the more you physically prompt a dog during early training, the harder it will be to achieve off-leash reliability later on.

EFFICIENCY   Physical prompting is deceptive because initially it appears that the dog is learning quickly. And he may be. He may quickly learn to sit when you pull up on the collar or push down on the rump, for example. However, it is not until the dog is off leash in the park that you learn you have barely started training. If your ultimate goal is verbal and distance control, physical prompting methods will at least double your training time because you will find that your dog responds only when on leash, when you can push and pull him about.

ENJOYMENT   Physical prompting is generally not very enjoyable for the dog. Who likes being pushed and pulled? If your dog doesn't enjoy training, it is much less likely that you will.

Training Techniques Go Full Circle

Until the last century, dog training was a pretty friendly affair. Dogs were predominantly trained by using reward methods. And of course, if we go even further back in time, food and gentleness were the ways we lured canines into the human family.

Unfortunately, the 1900s brought with it an array of confusing punishment-based dog-training techniques, and "Correct me if I'm wrong" became the mantra for the unassuming pet dog. Jerking on choke chains, yelling commands, and other menacing tactics became the hallmarks of popular, unfriendly dog-training methods. These techniques were harsh and demanding for both dogs and owners. Indeed, most dog owners found that the physical demands of these techniques were all but impossible to master. To better understand the dog-friendly approach, you need to understand where these punitive methods came from.

We're in the Army Now!

Perhaps pet dog trainers looked to military training methods for guidance. Obviously, military training techniques were intentionally harsh in an effort to weed out more sensitive dogs in the preliminary training, rather than having them break down in the field. Now, of course, most well-trained military dogs are trained by using fun and games and toys and treats. Fun and friendly dog training has even invaded the military!

And Now We're in the Woods?

The second factor that led to unfriendly, punishment-based training was an attempt to adopt the way wolves communicate to the dog-human training repertoire. This approach is severely flawed.

We first lured dogs into our lives by using food and kindness.

First, you don't look, smell, or growl like a dog, and you don't wear a furry costume and crawl around on all fours. The point is, it is impossible for people to communicate accurately in dog (or wolf) language.

Moreover, dogs and wolves have an extremely complicated social structure that is composed of a number of flexible hierarchies. As a dog owner, attempting to replicate this environment by attributing alpha ("top dog") status to yourself is a simplistic approach doomed to failure. Working from the inaccurate premise that wolves teach each other by using consistent and severe physical corrections, trainers devised an adversarial, combative training methodology. Rather than teaching our best friends, we were advised to physically dominate our dogs to bring them into line.

In actuality, very little physical force is required to maintain the social stability of a pack of wolves or dogs. Cooperation and passive gestures ensure that each member has access to resources (such as food) and ensures the pack's survival. If you really want to act like a wolf, forget the growling and scruff-shaking. Simply get control of the resources in your dog's life and show your dog what he should do to get them (such as sit, lie down, come when called, or eliminate outside). This approach is comparable to being a boss who is kind and gentle while making it clear that you are the one who signs the paychecks.

The Leash: A Good Tool Gone Bad

Yes, this simple, useful, and important training tool has had some unexpected and long-lasting negative side effects on training.

A mere fifty years ago, many dogs lived in areas where they could safely be off leash, but now the increased population density necessitates that dogs are walked on leash. Rather than developing the notion of staying close (an important aspect of any relationship), the dog was kept close by means of a leash. The leash also made it easy to jerk the dog around, and soon leash jerks became the universal correction, almost to the exclusion of people using their intelligence and creativity in training. Indeed, the easy implementation of punishment is a major reason leash training has gained such a bad reputation over the years. The final result? Dogs who became desensitized to leash jerks or didn't respond well to being bullied wound up being labeled stupid, stubborn, dominant, or aggressive.

Puppies Save the Day!

As people became dependent on physical and punitive training methods, it became almost impossible to train puppies. After all, you don't want to jerk, push, and pull a little puppy, do you? So people were advised to wait to train their puppies until they were 6 months old and could withstand the rigors of training. I certainly agree that puppies do not do well with punishment-based methods, but then neither do most adult dogs!

This approach, of course, is disastrous. Scientists have long realized how crucial a dog's early weeks of life are and suggest that waiting to train

Puppies prompted the turnaround to the friendly, positive direction of yesteryear. Gentle methods of training used to teach young puppies were so much fun and so effective that people began to use them with adult dogs.

until a dog is all but grown is just plain silly. Waiting until your pup is 6 months old to start teaching him how to behave is like waiting to start teaching your child the alphabet and numbers until she is in her teens.

Not training puppies made matters even worse, because by the time they hit adolescence, they were out of control. Owners were at their wits' end, resorting to almost any means—especially punishment—to gain control. Ironically, when they began to train their adolescent dogs, they used the same harsh methods they had originally avoided by not training at all!

Thanks go to veterinarian, animal behaviorist, and author Ian Dunbar, who brought puppy training back into fashion. By convincing people that they could and *should* teach their puppies when they're young and making training a fun endeavor, Dr. Dunbar revolutionized the life of dogs around the world. There is no doubt that dogs everywhere say a daily group thank-you to Dr. Dunbar. Certainly, before Dr. Dunbar's influence, you would have been hard pressed to find a puppy class, and there were precious few tail wags in training.

The impact of Dr. Dunbar's fun and friendly puppy classes was overwhelming. Fun and friendly training methods worked so well with puppies that people started to use them with adolescent and adult dogs. And they worked so well with adult dogs that people tried them out on fearful and aggressive dogs, too. And bingo! It turns out that friendly dog training is the method of choice for fearful and aggressive dogs. Naturally, fearsome and threatening methods are not the way to connect with fearful and threatened dogs.

As you can see by visiting a few puppy-training and dog-training classes in your area, fun and friendly dog training has all but taken over the dog world. Classes are filled with giggles and wagging tails; kids are involved; formal obedience competitions are getting a serious run for their money from events such as flyball, agility, and freestyle; and, most important, more dogs are learning how to be fun and friendly family members.

When to Begin Training?

Now! Right away! Using dog-friendly methods, it is never too early to train a puppy or a newly adopted adult dog. If you are planning to get a dog, read on. Reading this book will help you choose the best education for you and your dog.

Building a Bond with Your Dog

A good relationship with your dog means that he will look to you for guidance. This, rather than using physical force to dominate him, is the better way to become your dog's leader. A good relationship is the foundation of a great future for your dog. The more energy you focus on building this foundation, the less time you will spend resolving behavior issues. A teacher who fosters a safe and nurturing relationship with her students is most likely to help those students fulfill their potential as quickly as possible. A child would not be expected to thrive in a class with a teacher whom she fears and mistrusts, and neither can a pet dog.

A trusting and cooperative relationship is a requirement for dog-friendly dog training. By now, you should be convinced that dog-friendly dog training is the easiest, most efficient, and most enjoyable way to go. As a dog-friendly trainer, you are on your way to achieving your training goals, the most important of which is building a trusting bond between you and your dog. Actually, now that you have chosen to be a dog-friendly dog trainer, you have already all but done so. You have ensured that you and your dog will be good buddies because you will be using fun and friendly techniques to teach him.

Bonding with your dog couldn't be easier. Simply choose dog-friendly training methods (you've done that) and manage your dog's life so that you give him the best chance to be right.

Training opens up communication channels between you and your dog. Yes! It is possible to talk to the animals.

Jump-Starting the Relationship

The best way to jump-start the relationship with your dog is to hand-feed him. Get your dog's bowl off the floor, sit down, and chat with him. Just as studies have shown the importance of families eating at least one meal together a day, the same is true with respect to your relationship with your dog.

So, for at least one week, set aside five to ten minutes to hand-feed your dog his meal. Use each piece of food to ask him to sit, lie down, stand, roll over, or come. Also practice gentling and handling exercises. Offer him a piece of kibble each time you reach out to touch a part of his body. (See Chapter 6.)

With each piece of food your dog takes from your hand, you are cementing his trust and bond with you. Consider each piece like a deposit in the bank that will earn you an enormous amount of "interest" over your dog's life.

2

Tools to Help You Teach

Tools to help you train your dog are both concrete (things that you make or buy) and conceptual (methods). Tools include collars, leashes, toys, and treats as well as taking your dog for a walk as a reward for sitting when you ask and limiting your dog's access to your home until she has learned good manners.

Consider all the tools (both concrete and conceptual) that are at your disposal in your virtual trainer's toolbox. A well-stocked toolbox is a necessity for any reward-based trainer. Wisely chosen training aids will help you set your dog up for success and reward her for appropriate behaviors. Training aids also serve to enrich your dog's life, not only by keeping her mentally and physically stimulated but also by creating a dog who enjoys a peaceful and contented life with you since she so clearly understands what you want.

While a visit to your local pet supply store can be a thrilling adventure for you and your dog, it can also seem daunting if your goal is to pinpoint the best tools for training. As reward-based training has become the rule, the marketplace has been flooded with an almost endless assortment of products to help you excel at setting your dog up for success and rewarding her for behaviors you want to reinforce. Here are some tips on how to narrow your search so that you can create a great trainer's toolbox to aid in managing and enriching your dog's life.

Rewards

Rewards are the most powerful tools in training. They are the best way to say to your dog, "I like what you're doing." Rewards are also the best way to keep your dog happy and interested in learning from you, and to make training fun for your dog, you, your family, and your friends. Rewards are at the heart of dog-friendly dog training.

Listen to the Experts

Discoveries in the fields of psychology and education have had an incredible impact on all types of training: training children to be more focused and interested in the classroom, training employees to be more productive in the workplace, training families to communicate successfully, and, of course, training animals. Research has shown that positive reinforcement, not punishment, is the more effective approach. These findings were all but ignored in popular pet dog training until about the 1980s.

By definition, a reward is anything your dog likes. It can be a kind word, a scratch behind the ear, a walk in the park, a toss of a toy, or a bit of food. The list of possible rewards is endless, but it is important to keep in mind that each dog has unique preferences, just like we do. You should have a good idea of what your dog's favorite rewards are. In fact, I recommend that you make a list of your dog's top ten favorites. You will find that using your dog's favorite rewards for new, more complicated, or difficult behaviors (such as teaching your dog to come when called while playing in a dog run) is a wise way to make the most of these tools.

Behavioral Cement

Each time you reward your dog, you make her more likely to repeat what she was doing when or immediately before you rewarded her. For example, give your dog a treat when she sits to greet you, and she will be more likely to do so again. Each time you reward her for greeting you politely, you strengthen that behavior (and weaken inappropriate greeting behaviors, such as jumping up). Also, you strengthen your relationship with your dog because you have shown her what makes you happy, and by rewarding her you have made her happy as well.

Each and every reward increases your dog's eagerness to want to do what you want her to do.

Just as concrete reinforces the foundation of a building, rewards reinforce the foundation of your relationship with your dog by increasing the frequency of behaviors you like. By rewarding good behavior, you are cementing the relationship between you and your dog.

Endless Opportunities to Reward

The list of rewards for your dog is endless. It's a good thing there are so many different rewards, because using dog-friendly training methods means that you have endless opportunities to reward your dog.

Teach Your Dog to Say "Please"

Asking your dog to say "please" (for example, to sit) for dinner, for couch privileges, to go outside, or to play is one of the secrets of successful pet dog training.

For example, a single trip to the park is an opportunity to reward your dog many times. Take the leash in your hand and wait for your dog to sit before putting it on. Take just one step forward and wait for your dog to sit again. Continue a few steps at a time (stopping for sits) until you get to the door. As always, before going through doors, wait for your dog to sit and then open the door and/or give her a little treat. Go to your car (a few steps at a time) and wait for your dog to sit before opening the car door. Once at the park, wait for your dog to sit before letting her out of your vehicle. Wait for your dog to sit before letting her off leash (if it is safe to do so) and telling her to go play. Let your dog romp around for a while and then call her back to sit for a treat. When your dog sits, tell her "Go play" again and toss a ball for her.

Repeat this process many times as your dog investigates and plays. Every time you interrupt your dog's activities by asking her to come and sit, you can tell her to "Go play" once more. By doing so, play becomes a reward, which reinforces obedience rather than becoming a distraction that would compete with obedience. So many rewards at your disposal during just one trip to the park!

Don't Be Stingy!

While you should certainly vary when and what you give your dog, don't be stingy about giving rewards, especially when you are starting to teach something new. Think of yourself as a generous (but varied) slot machine. Rewarding generously means that the behaviors you like will be strongly reinforced and therefore more likely to become habit.

Turn Your Dog into a Gambler

The great thing about using rewards to train is that they are most effective when given inconsistently. This is convenient, too, because most of us are inconsistent in our behavior!

To understand the effectiveness of inconsistent rewards, you simply need to watch a gambler in front of a slot machine. She will spend a lot of time playing the machine, even if the machine spits out only a few rewards. What is the glue that keeps her there? Inconsistent rewards! The gambler is hooked on playing the game because a big part of the fun is the expectation of a jackpot and the thrill of not knowing when the next reward will appear.

A dog trained using dog-friendly methods is hooked on training like a gambler is hooked on gambling because you keep her guessing about when she will be rewarded and how valuable the reward will be (food, praise, a walk, or a ride in the car). In essence, you are your dog's reward slot machine!

Jackpot!

Randomly rewarding your dog for behaviors you like will keep her hooked on playing the training game with you. Adding an occasional "jackpot" reward, one that's extra-special, makes the game even more interesting and fun for you both. For example, when my dogs run to me especially fast when called, I make a bigger, happier fuss than usual.

Choosing Rewards

Your choice of what reward to use will depend on personal preference and, more important, on what works best for your dog. Know which rewards are your dog's favorites and realize that this preference may change from day to day, and even from minute to minute. For example, if you have been playing fetch for ten minutes, this game might not be a high priority for your dog for a while. So try something different.

It's a good idea to write down a list of your dog's favorite rewards ranked from one to ten. When you are working on new, more difficult, or very important behaviors (like coming when called) or in new or more distracting environments, you might use some of the highest-ranked rewards. Once your dog has learned something, vary the rewards as much as possible. Remember, variety is the spice of life and the secret to a well-trained dog. Nothing is more boring than eating the same old lunch day after day, or watching the same movie every night. Being inventive with what and how often you offer rewards is the best way to keep your dog interested in playing the training game.

These Are a Few of My Favorite Things

List your dog's favorite rewards and make the best use of the ones at the top of the list by saving them for times when she is learning something new or when she does something really special, like coming to you quickly when you call her. My dogs' favorites are:

- ✦ Special food treats
- ✦ Food-stuffed toys
- ✦ Squeaky toys
- ✦ Going for a walk
- ✦ Playing fetch
- ✦ Invitations onto the bed
- ✦ Being petted
- ✦ Verbal praise
- ✦ Playing with other dogs
- ✦ Playing on our agility course

Verbal Praise

Verbal praise such as "Good dog" or "Who's a terrific pup?" is the first thing most people think of as a reward. Words are especially useful rewards because you always have your voice with you, and you can use it to reward your dog from a distance!

Believe it or not, you may need to teach your dog that your voice means something good. Dogs don't start off understanding that human praise is a good thing, and some dogs' early experiences in life actually make them wary of human voices (for example, as a result of being verbally reprimanded). Spend a week or so hand-feeding your dog part of her meals and talking to her, telling her that she is a good girl as you offer each piece. This way, she will learn to associate your voice with something all dogs like—food. You won't always have to give a treat after praising her, because eventually the praise itself will become rewarding.

Attention and Affection

Petting, scratching, and massaging are wonderful rewards for most dogs. This is great, because physical contact is one of the most enjoyable aspects of living with a dog.

Attention and affection are especially good positive feedback for lengthy behaviors (such as a long down—see Chapter 7) and, of course, for teaching your dog to relax and enjoy handling, examination, and restraint. As a bonus, grooming, attention, and affection are equally relaxing for you, the trainer!

Be aware that attention and affection are also effective at unintentionally encouraging inappropriate and unwanted behaviors. For example, if you pet your dog when she whines and giggle when she jumps up on you, you are training her to do both. All you have to do is reserve attention and affection for times when your dog is well behaved.

Some dogs may become overexcited when people touch them. If your dog is like this, either reserve hands-on petting for when your dog has a good foundation of training and impulse control (covered in Chapter 6) or use gentle, slow, rhythmic petting to soothe and calm your dog.

Toys, Activities, and Games

You can play a limitless number of games with your dog. Active games like chasing a tennis ball or toy, playing tug, or playing hide-and-seek are terrific, but so are quieter games, like a family competition to see who can get your dog to lie down quietly for the longest time for a single piece of kibble.

You have a huge variety of toys to choose from, including food-stuffable toys, squeaky toys, tug toys, and balls. To figure out which toys your dog likes best, take your dog with you to the pet store and see if she shows a particular interest. Better yet, take her to visit friends with friendly dogs and see if she especially likes any of their toys. This is also a great way to maintain your dog's socialization (see Chapter 4).

My favorite toys for dogs are hollow toys that can be stuffed with a variety of foods, including your dog's normal dry or wet food as well as special treats. These toys should be all but indestructible (which means that they will last a very long time). Squeaky toys are great, but I suggest allowing your dog to play with them only when you are there to supervise. Squeaky toys are generally easy to tear apart, and your dog could choke on some of the parts. Ropes and other tug toys are also good items to have in your reward repertoire, but they should be used for supervised play and only if you can ask your dog to let go of the toy and she does so without a fuss. (Later on I'll talk about teaching your dog to share.) Toys are

Rewarding your dog with affection and games is as pleasant for you as it is for your dog.

magically effective for training your dog to train herself when you are not around. For example, if you stuff a toy with your dog's food, your dog will teach herself to play with her toy and not your shoes!

Make toys a valuable reward by controlling your dog's access to them. If your dog has ten toys lying around the house, chances are none of them will work as an effective reward for very long. That is, if there is an ample supply of something, the demand is likely to be lower. But if you leave just a couple of stuffed chew toys out at a time and put the rest away, you will find that when you do take them out, your dog will be very interested in them. She'll also want to know what you'd like her to do in order to get them! So ask her to come, sit, lie down, or otherwise earn these items.

Food for Thought

Food is one of the most perfect rewards! It works with every dog (every dog needs to eat), it is quick (especially soft, easy-to-chew types), it is easy to carry, and it is a wonderful way to gauge your dog's mood (a fearful or highly stressed dog is less likely to eat). Food is especially convenient and easy to use during initial training, as it takes just a moment to reward your dog with a tiny treat that can be eaten quickly so that you can move right on to more training exercises. This is immensely

Fetch is one of the best activities to enjoy with your dog, and it's a great way to practice sit (before the toy is tossed), come (as she runs to bring it back to you), and give (when she lets you have the toy back to toss again).

valuable considering that repetition is the key to building physical and learning muscles.

Moreover, offering a tiny bit of food enables you to pinpoint a moment of good behavior with precise timing. This is one of the reasons so many dogs working in movies and on television are trained using food as one of their primary rewards. Food is essential for keeping most dogs, especially those who must perform complicated behaviors, happy and reliable.

In my training classes, some people express concerns about using food as a training tool. It's difficult to understand people's misgivings about food in training, especially since it makes training so easy and effective. These criticisms are generally unfounded and can be more accurately directed toward other training tools: for example, the all-too-common leash correction. However, in the case of using food, these concerns are baseless. The chart on pages 52–53 sets out the most common concerns about using food rewards and how they can be answered.

Be sure to offer tiny treats as rewards so you can practice many repetitions. It is better to practice ten sits for tiny rewards than one sit for a large treat.

The Great Food Debate

For some strange reason, the use of food in training has become a controversial issue. Before we take any anti-food sentiments too seriously, perhaps we should consider how humans domesticated the dog in the first place. Basically, Mr. Caveman got wild animals to keep their distance by yelling at them, but he lured wolves to come close by tossing them little morsels of—dare I say it?—food!

Remember, ask your dog to sit (or down, stand, roll over, etc.) before every privilege and pleasurable activity—for example, a ride in the car to go to the park.

Life Rewards

Simple rewards such as toys, treats, and petting are especially effective for pinpointing good behavior during initial training. And, like all rewards, toys, treats, and petting remain a wonderful permanent ingredient in the lifelong relationship between you and your dog, even after your dog is trained. But you will find that as your dog matures and develops her interests, some of the best rewards are relevant *life rewards*—allowing your dog to do what she wants as a reward for good behavior. These can be passive activities like being invited up on the couch, active events like continuing a walk or throwing a disc, or mind-blowing events like a trip to the park or the beach.

Concerns about Using Food	The Facts about Using Food	Equivalent Concerns about Using Punishment
I don't want to use food in training because then my dog will respond only when I have food to offer her.	There are many ways to decrease the use of food (or any reward) in training. Food lures are replaced by verbal cues and hand signals. Food rewards are sometimes replaced with motivating life rewards, such as activities and games, and are offered only on a random schedule.	I don't want to use a leash in training because my dog will be obedient only when she's on leash.
Isn't it demeaning to use treats during training?	Let's get the dog's opinion on this one! Personally, I love using food, and my dogs love when I use it, too.	Isn't it demeaning to push, pull, squish, squash, and jerk your dog in training?
Isn't using food just bribing your dog?	I don't want to bribe my dogs because, as most parents and politicians know, bribes seldom work in the long run. But rewards? They are a different matter. Don't you look forward to payday at the end of the month? What's wrong with paying a dog for a job well done?	Isn't using physical punishment just unpleasant and hurtful?

Concerns about Using Food	The Facts about Using Food	Equivalent Concerns about Using Punishment
If I train my dog using food, won't she get fat?	Not if you use good sense. Try weighing out your dog's food in the morning, putting it in a container, and using it periodically throughout the day as rewards. No extra calories, but a whole lot of potential rewards. Even when you do use special treats, your dog is unlikely to gain weight if you ration them out thoughtfully and provide your dog with adequate exercise.	If I use leash corrections, won't my dog get hurt and scared?
What if my dog doesn't care about food?	If your dog is not enthusiastic about food, you can train her to have a greater interest in earning her food by spending one week hand-feeding her at least part of her meals. But in reality, almost all puppies and most adult dogs will readily work for food, especially for special treats.	What if my dog doesn't care for punishment and shuts down from learning in anticipation of being punished?
What if food overexcites my dog?	The only efficient way to teach a dog not to touch food on the table, counter, or hand until given permission is to use food in training and when working on impulse control, both as a distraction and as a reward.	What if getting the leash makes my dog go crazy with anticipation of a walk?

Your dog will find many things in the environment rewarding. For example, two of my dogs' favorites are smells and squirrels. Instead of trying to compete with such valuable rewards (what some might call distractions), I use them to my benefit. On a typical walk in the park, I ask my dogs to sit or lie down a number of times. Occasionally, I reward them by releasing them to spend a few minutes sniffing a particularly enticing spot, or let them have an intense staring contest with one of the resident squirrels.

The Ultimate Reward

Dogs obviously enjoy reward training. They love praise, petting, toys, treats, and all the fun and games. Better yet, in no time at all, dogs come to enjoy the actual training activities. Indeed, for a reward-trained dog, the very best rewards are the actions and activities themselves.

Train your dog well, and then the best reward for walking nicely by your side is that your dog gets to walk by your side.

Your dog now runs to you quickly because she likes to run to you quickly. She walks by your side because that's her favorite place to be and you are her favorite friend. Training that is built on gentle guidance, good communication, and oodles of rewards results in training itself becoming the ultimate reward.

Once your dog has been reward trained, she will eventually require very little external reinforcement or motivation, since she enjoys playing the training game just as much as you do.

Consequences for Inappropriate Behavior
Removal of Rewards

Removing the things your dog likes best is an extremely effective way to respond to inappropriate behavior. For example, if your dog is not giving you her full attention, show her the reward she could have won, whether it is a piece of food, a tennis ball, or a toy, and tell her, "Silly dog, you could have won this, but now you can't have it." Put it away, sit down, and read a book. After a few minutes, try again, and you will probably find that your dog has better focus and an improved attitude. She will see the value in paying attention to you. This is a great opportunity to remind her that you hold the key to her "resource treasure chest."

When you begin training your dog, keeping her on leash where you can supervise her, whether indoors or out, is the best way to get the maximum value from rewards (and their removal). This way, your dog can't just go off to look for fun elsewhere. Essentially, by controlling her access to resources and the environment, you make yourself more valuable. The leash can be tethered to a stable object (such as the couch you are sitting on), or you can step on the end of it or hold it in your hand to keep your dog from wandering about. Be sure she has at least two food-stuffed toys to keep her busy.

Because training soon becomes one of a reward-trained dog's favorite activities, time out from training is the ultimate punishment. Time out means no more training, no more rewards, and no more trainer (the person your dog most wants to be with!). After a short break, your dog comes back refocused on spending time with you and on the wonderful benefits

When a time-out is your best punishment, you know that you have a great relationship with your dog and you are training the right way.

of interacting with you—play, treats, and toys. During the initial stages of training, having your dog on leash while you supervise her gives you a calm way of giving a time-out by holding the leash gently at arm's length, stepping on the leash to keep your dog in one spot, using it to walk her calmly to her crate or long-term confinement area, or tethering the leash to a stable object.

During the early stages of training, you can simply ignore your dog for a minute or two when she is tethered to a stable object a few feet away from you, put her in her long-term or short-term confinement area (discussed in Chapter 3), or actually leave the room. Note that when you begin training a very young pup, you should make a point of playing with and training your dog in her long-term confinement area so that it is safe for you to leave your dog alone immediately. Better yet, have your dog on leash so that all you have to do is stand up, step on the leash or hold it at arm's length, and ignore her.

If you have two dogs, you can ignore the inattentive dog and offer your other dog numerous rewards. Not only does this approach relieve your frustration, but it is also the best way to get your inattentive dog's attention.

Remember, after a time-out, instruct your dog to do something, such as come and sit, to reestablish your control and give her the opportunity to get back to playing the training game with you.

Become a Great Reward Manipulator

Focus on reinforcing your dog's behavior by manipulating rewards. This is without a doubt the best way to train. You show the dog what you want her to do and then reward her when she does it. The best way to inhibit and eliminate unwanted behavior is to train your dog to want to do what you want. For example, teach your dog to sit and ask her to do so when she greets you. If she is sitting, she can't be jumping on you! If your dog doesn't comply, the best "punishment" is a temporary time-out from you, training, and rewards.

Instructive Redirection

Many punishments do not have the desired effect because they are not instructive. They often simply confuse the dog and, in some cases, make her shut down out of frustration or fear, which is not a good state of mind when you are trying to teach her. Letting your dog know that she has made a mistake is not sufficient. Sure, your dog knows that you are upset, but what should she do to make things right? If you want your dog to learn what she should be doing, you must be instructive. "Get your toy!" is far more effective than "NO! Bad dog!" If your dog is about to eliminate indoors, the exclamation "Let's go outside!" informs your dog where it is appropriate to go rather than scaring her with a "NO! Bad dog!"

Similarly, if you think your dog might jump up on visitors, simply instruct your dog to "Sit" rather than scream "No!" or "Aaargh!" or "Off!" once she has. Take this incident as a reminder that your dog is not yet ready to greet visitors off leash. So put the leash on when you bring her to the door to say hello and step on it so it is short enough that she can't jump.

Although screaming "No!" may startle the dog into non-activity for a moment, the dog is still not doing what you want, and she is likely to become more frantic (due partly to the stress of having been yelled at) and may go right back to doing what you don't like again. Anyway, telling the dog what you want her to do is much easier on the dog and much more effective. This way, you are truly correcting in that you are helping your dog to be correct.

It's also important to teach your dog that tone and volume signal urgency, not the prospect of pain or punishment. Think of how you would want your dog to react in an emergency. If she gets off leash and starts to run across a busy street, you will probably panic and yell at her. If she thinks this means she's in trouble, she may run away from you and get hurt.

Booby Traps

Booby traps may be effective occasionally, but they are still unpleasant (by definition), and most store-bought booby traps and alarm systems are very expensive. It is much easier and more effective to prevent your dog from misbehaving (confinement and supervision) and teach her an acceptable alternative behavior. For example, providing a little occupational therapy, such as a stuffed toy in your dog's crate, will work better than booby traps all over your house to stop her from chewing inappropriate objects.

Yelling at your dog really only teaches her that you are enjoying training as little as she is. Why not just calmly show her what you would like her to do and reward her for doing so?

Non-Instructive Reprimands (Not Advised)

Continually harping after your dog "No! Bad dog!" with high volume, a nasty tone, and an ugly face just tells your dog that you don't like her. But you *do* like your dog; it is merely her behavior that you consider to be unacceptable.

Many owners lose it when reprimanding their dogs and end up yelling emotionally. Being yelled at is stressful. Like people, dogs have a hard time learning when under stress, so it's unlikely that your dog will learn much (other than to be fearful of you) in the midst of your tirade. Why are you yelling? Your dog is not deaf! And if she is deaf, she can't hear you! So, please, stop yelling. Instead, take a deep breath and look at the situation from the perspective of "What can I do to change this situation and set my dog up to be successful?" If your dog is raiding the kitchen garbage can, for example, get a can with a lid that your dog can't penetrate, or find a way to prevent your dog from having unsupervised access to the kitchen.

Negative Reinforcement (Not Advised)

Negative reinforcement is the negation (or stopping) of punishment to reinforce appropriate behavior. An example would be using a shock collar to cause pain until your dog starts to run in your direction, at which point the shock is stopped. This is, of course, extremely unpleasant for your dog (and you), and it often brings with it very serious negative side effects, such as fear and potentially aggression. This approach puts you on thin ice regarding your dog's temperament. Indeed, many dogs crack when negative reinforcement is applied.

It's Great to Be Good!

A dog who is trained with dog-friendly methods will make many good decisions because she is counting on the potential reinforcement and because she has a history of being rewarded for those choices. In this case, you have a wonderful dog and should be proud that she got that way because she was rewarded for "good" behaviors instead of being punished for "bad" behaviors. If you train your dog not to do "bad" things because she may get caught and get in trouble, don't be surprised if she looks for those opportunities when she won't get caught. Your dog-friendly–trained dog won't look for opportunities to get away with "bad" behaviors because she will be too busy looking for opportunities to bring about pleasant consequences.

Physical Punishment (Definitely Not Advised)

This is definitely not how you want to treat your best friend. Most disturbingly, physical punishment is almost always non-instructive—the dog has no idea why she is being abused and is under serious stress while the punishment is happening. Like us, a dog is not equipped to learn much when overwhelmed with fear. Harsh physical punishment is totally inappropriate, uncalled for, and utterly unacceptable in pet dog training.

The Side Effects of Punishment

Harsh physical or verbal punishments are relatively ineffective and may cause a number of serious side effects on the dog's temperament and on your relationship. Even when punishment training seems to have been effective in resolving simple behavior problems, it invariably shakes the dog's confidence and undermines the trusting relationship between trainer and dog.

Punishments administered by the owner quickly become associated with both the owner and the training process. The result? The dog may learn to comply, grudgingly and perhaps only temporarily, but she also has begun to learn to dislike training—and the trainer.

For example, when a dog has been punished for jumping up, she may not jump up at the moment, but she probably likes the owner and greeting people just a little bit less. The trainer has won the battle but lost the war. The dog may become progressively more fearful with each punishment. If the dog ever expresses dislike for training, the "stubborn" dog will be punished more severely. And if the dog ever decides to correct the trainer for a poor choice in training techniques by growling or biting, the poor dog will most likely be more severely punished and possibly banished from her home.

One of the most common problems associated with punishment-based techniques is that many pet dogs quickly become desensitized to corrections, causing the owner to resort to stronger and stronger corrective actions. Gentle tugs on a buckle collar become firmer jerks on a metal choke collar, which are then replaced with even firmer yanks on a spiked metal "pinch" collar or zaps from an electric shock collar. The poor dog suffers because her owner did not fully understand a technique that at its best is severely flawed. Because dogs are social animals, they are often only too willing to put up with high-level punishment if only to be allowed to remain part of a social group. High-tech pain-delivery equipment is not the solution to the problems we have with our dogs.

No-No's

Rather than yelling "No!" at your dog when she does something you don't like, why not give her a little constructive criticism? For example, if she is jumping, tell her to sit. If she seems to be looking for something to chew, give her a toy so that she doesn't try out a table leg.

Finally, using punishment-based techniques is the best way to create behavior problems when you're not at home. For example, after just one or two punishments for chewing inappropriate objects or eliminating in the wrong spot, the dog would no doubt become a closet chewer or eliminator, reserving her chewing and elimination activities for times when her owner is away. Your dog will wait until you leave to do things because then you, "the punisher," are not there to punish. Think about when you exceed the speed limit. If you see a police car, you slow down, but you'll continue to speed if you think you can get away with it. The same philosophy applies to your dog. If you punish her when you are there, she'll learn to behave in certain ways when you are not there. Your dog is not misbehaving out of spite; she's simply acting like a dog when she feels that it's safe to do so—that is, when the big, bad punisher is not around.

And punishment is time-consuming. You have to be present to punish your dog. Most people cannot and do not want to stay home all day so that they can constantly reprimand their dogs. As a result, punishment is often administered after the dog has already misbehaved, which is not only unpleasant and ineffective, but also means that the dog has been allowed to practice behaviors you don't like. Why not just train the dog to chew one chew toy instead?

It cannot be overemphasized that the main focus of pet dog training is to teach dogs what you think is right, not to punish them for what you think is wrong. Without a doubt, this is the easiest, most efficient, most effective, and indeed the most enjoyable way to teach your dog.

Training Tools to Buy

Lots of tools can help you train your dog. In fact, there are so many options that making a choice can be quite confusing! Really, though, you need only a few basics to get started. You can add to your toolbox as your training progresses and you have a better idea of what your dog's favorite rewards and activities are.

Buckle Collar

Your dog needs a buckle collar, as it is essential for safety that she wear identification at all times, and ID tags can be most conveniently attached to a buckle collar. Similarly, a buckle collar offers a convenient attachment for your dog's leash, so you can safely walk your dog and train her in open areas.

Head Halter

A head halter is a wonderful, humane alternative to a pain-inducing collar. A halter affords the owner a considerable mechanical advantage to manage the dog. Whether the dog is strong and active or very tiny, a head halter can be a wonderful training aid.

Head halters work on the age-old horsey premise that it's easier to lead an animal by her head than by her neck. There are a variety of halters on the market, each with its own innovations. When used correctly, these halters offer almost instantaneous control of rambunctious or untrained dogs.

A head halter is the physical equivalent of luring a dog with a food treat. Lead her by her head and the body will follow.

At first, your dog might find that this collar feels a bit strange (much in the same way that puppies react when first fitted with a buckle collar). To make the adjustment as easy as possible, simply spend one or two meals hand-feeding your dog her food as you put the halter on and take it off. Then stand up and entice your dog to walk with you by luring her with a piece of food. Walk smoothly, without jerking on the leash or stopping, and frequently reward your dog for walking with you. Before you know it, your dog will be happy to have the halter on because it signals the beginning of a delightful walk (which you will do more often now that your dog is so much easier to control).

Looks Can Be Deceiving

Unfortunately, halter-type collars are sometimes mistaken for muzzles, creating an image problem for these handy tools. But don't let their looks bother you. They are gentle aids and work like a dream!

The Reward/Reprimand Rainbow

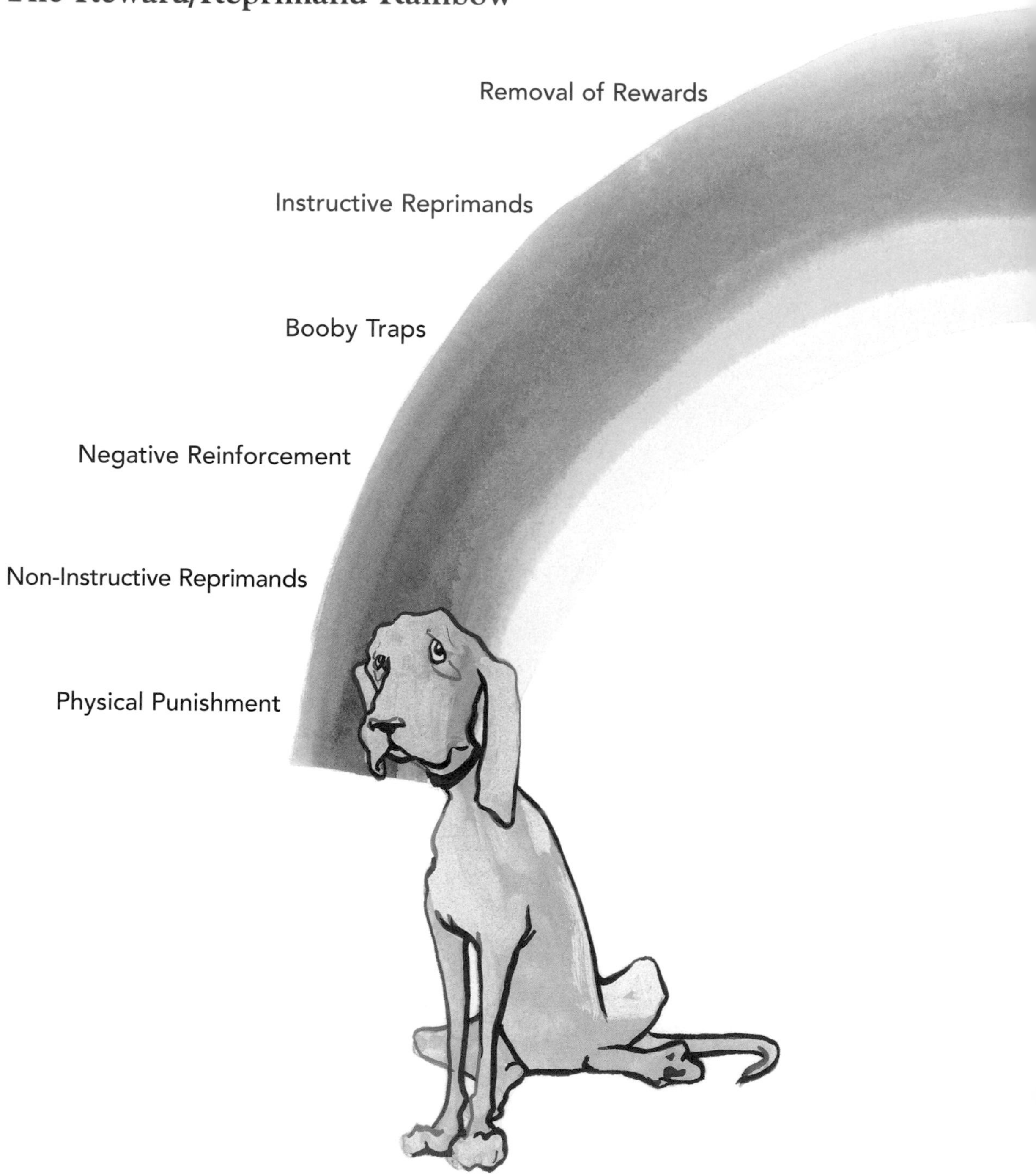

Removal of Rewards

Instructive Reprimands

Booby Traps

Negative Reinforcement

Non-Instructive Reprimands

Physical Punishment

Verbal Praise

Attention and Affection

Toys, Activities, and Games

Treats

Life Rewards

Internal Motivation

Don't make your dog blue.
Reward your dog for getting it right.

Leashes

There are two basic options in the leash department: a standard 3- to 6-foot nylon or leather leash and a retractable leash. I strongly recommend using a standard leash until your dog has learned to walk nicely by your side. A retractable leash is useful for giving a dog a wider area to roam, but nothing encourages a dog to pull more than allowing constant tension in the leash. This is the case with retractable leashes. These leashes may not be as safe as a standard 3- to 6-foot leash, either, as your dog may get so far ahead of or behind you that she turns a corner without you and

Would you ever try to jerk a bear around?

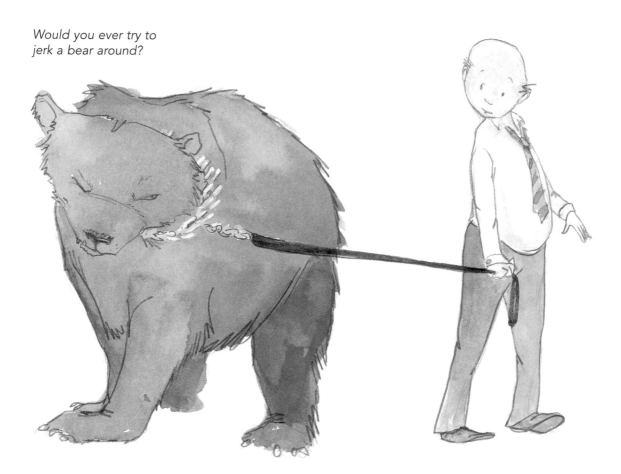

comes upon another dog or some hazard. Also, the plastic handle of a retractable leash can slip out of your hand, and if it falls to the ground it could scare your dog and cause her to run.

The greatest benefit of leash training is safety. A leashed dog can safely be trained on the street, which is convenient because you want to be able to take your dog for walks on the street. Leash training also facilitates adult dog-training classes, which are generally conducted with dogs on leash. The leash offers control and safety, which may be easily incorporated into reward-based training methods.

The Leash Gets a Bum Rap

Leash training has gained a bad reputation because so many people associate leashes with collar corrections and punishments. This is too bad, because some aspects (such as safety) are extremely beneficial.

The leash is a wonderful training tool to help your dog settle down and walk calmly on leash. Simply tie the leash to an immovable object and your dog will soon settle down. Even better, tie your dog's leash and give her a food-stuffed toy. Before you know it, she will learn to settle down quietly and chew her chew toy.

For the leash to be effective, it doesn't have to be used punitively. Walking your dog on leash is comparable to holding a child's hand for gentle guidance. When walking a child on a busy city street, you hold his hand for safety. You don't hold hands to hurt or cause pain. Think of a leash in the same way—a convenient means to hold your dog's "hand." Simply focus on using the leash passively (to gently guide and prevent unwanted behaviors) rather than actively (to jerk your dog around). Use the leash, but do not abuse the leash. Use it for safety and for occasional motivational prompting, but don't use it to cause pain or administer harsh punishment.

And remember: No matter how well trained you think your dog is, when outdoors keep her on leash unless you are absolutely sure that it is safe for her to be off leash.

The Four C's of Leash Safety

1. Common sense
2. Control
3. Courtesy to others
4. Catastrophe prevention

Clicker

A *clicker* is a small, handheld device that makes a distinct "click" sound when you press it. Repetitive pairing of the clicker sound with a reinforcer such as food makes the sound become what is called a *conditioned reinforcer*. In simple terms, this means you have taught your dog that the sound of the click means food (or some other reinforcer) is coming. The clicker is a fantastic way of letting your dog know that what she did at the *exact* moment the click happened is what earned her the reward. Many of my students also like to teach a verbal marker, such as the word "yes," which, like the clicker, is repetitively paired with a food reward until the dog understands that hearing this word means that what she did at that *exact* moment earned her a reward. Both markers are useful. While a verbal marker is something you always have with you, many professional trainers prefer a clicker because it makes a distinct and unique sound.

A clicker provides you a way to accurately pinpoint behaviors.

Crate

A crate is one of the most useful tools for just about every aspect of training. It is a valuable aid for housetraining, chew-toy training, and teaching your dog to calmly accept time alone, and it can be a wonderful convenience when you travel with your pet.

There are two basic kinds of crates: plastic and metal. I generally prefer plastic crates because they tend to make less noise (a dog moving about in a metal crate can be quite noisy) and tend to be more calming environments. Plastic crates are generally more appropriate for travel, and this slightly more enclosed structure may help increase your dog's sense of comfort and safety.

Confining a dog to a crate with a stuffed chew toy is like confining a child to his room with a video game or a good book or a baby to her crib with fun toys!

The crate should be sized appropriately for your dog. It should be just large enough for your dog to stand up, turn around, and lie down in. Keep in mind that if you buy a crate for your young puppy, you may need a larger size when she grows up. A cost-efficient solution is to buy a large crate and block off part of it until your puppy grows into it.

Bear in mind that a crate is a temporary tool. Your dog may have full run of the house once she understands the rules, but you'll probably find that your dog will still choose to go to her crate when she wants peace and quiet.

Chew Toys

Every dog should have at least ten hollow, food-stuffable chew toys. Rotate the toys, giving your dog at least two to four freshly stuffed toys each day. When you are home and can supervise your dog, she can chew by your side or in her crate (until she is trained, and then she can chew anywhere in your home she is permitted). If you have to leave, let her settle comfortably in her confinement area with a few good chew toys.

Most dogs will immediately become engrossed in a food-stuffed toy, especially if you are a creative stuffer. Try lots of different fillings to find which ones your dog likes best. Use just a small bit of filling and make it tough for your dog to get at it. You can also freeze the food-stuffed toy. Your dog will spend her day enjoyably engrossed in the task of trying to get to the center of her chew toys.

Creating a chew-toy habit in your dog may save you and your dog more grief and aggravation than you can possibly imagine. The list of "wrong" things your dog can do to keep herself occupied (both when you are home and especially while you are away) is endless. However, the list of "right" things your pet dog can do in your home is pretty short, especially when you aren't home. Teaching your dog to do one "right" thing is

Chew toys?

Or total household destruction?

obviously much easier and less time-consuming than teaching her not to do an endless list of wrongs.

Even the smallest dog can do a lot of damage to a home in a very short period. Damage done by chewing alone can be immense. But you can't expect to stop your dog from chewing altogether. After all, chewing is one of the few pet dog hobbies we deem acceptable. All you have to do is teach your dog *what* to chew. The quickest and easiest solution to many potential problems is to make your dog a chew toy–aholic!

Ideally, your dog should eat all of her meals out of these toys. This way, she has an appropriate outlet for her physical and mental energy. An adult dog who eats her food out of a bowl in five minutes is left with a great deal of time with nothing to do for the rest of the day. Instead, you can enrich your dog's life by having her "hunt" for her food from food-stuffed toys.

Paws to Consider

Your dog's crate and chew toys are most effective when used together. Put a food-stuffed toy in your dog's crate before you leave and close the crate door with your dog out of the crate. This way, she will become occupied with getting into it, not with your imminent departure. The old saying "You always want what you can't have" is at play here. When you open the door a minute or two later, chances are she will dive right in.

Given the lack of "Working Retriever Wanted" ads in the employment section of your local paper, don't be surprised if your dog ends up carrying any and every item that is not nailed to the wall around in her mouth. Play fetch with appropriate objects (toys). Then your dog will know that only certain things are meant to be played with.

If you catch your dog in the act of chewing an inappropriate article, do not resort to yelling at her. Reprimanding her is the quickest way to develop an owner-absent chewing problem. She will learn to wait until you are gone to chew. Ultimately, you want her to chew only appropriate items regardless of your presence. Think about supervising her when you're home and confining her to her area (a crate, an exercise pen, or a room that has been puppy-proofed) with some good chew toys when you can't keep your eye on her.

Don't give your puppy or dog any items to chew on that resemble items you don't want her to chew on. A dog can't distinguish your worn-out tennis shoes from a brand-new pair. And don't give your dog real bones that have been cooked. Once cooked, the bones soften and can splinter easily. Bone splinters can injure your dog's mouth and stomach.

Special Puppy Chew-Toy Considerations

Between the ages of 3 and 6 months, your puppy will lose her baby teeth as her adult teeth grow in. During this time, your puppy will experience discomfort, and chewing will help to alleviate it. Make sure that your puppy always has an appropriate chew toy available, especially during this teething period. Some puppies like to chew on ice cubes or food-stuffed chew toys that have been frozen, which may help to numb the discomfort of teething.

Let Your Dog Act a Little Wild

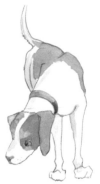

In the wild, dogs spend 80 percent of their waking hours searching for food. But we put the same food in the same bowl in the same place every day. Make life a little more fun for your dog! Hide her dinner in a toy or, better yet, in a few different toys, and give your dog a chance to act like a dog again by "hunting" for her food.

Training Tools You Won't Need

Devices designed to cause discomfort and pain exist because people believe that high-tech equipment is the cure-all for our dogs' problems. But most expensive gadgets don't offer a magic remedy. In reality, a better understanding of reward training is the answer. Resorting to extreme physical measures to train dogs just advertises that the trainer has neither understood nor applied the much more effective reward-based training techniques.

Even when used correctly, painful punishment tools have significant side effects. These side effects often have disastrous consequences for the relationship between dog and owner. Work on training your dog in a friendly way instead.

How Dogs Learn

Understanding how dogs learn provides many useful clues regarding how best to teach them and which tools to use to do so. Dogs' thought is neither inferior nor superior to ours; it's just different. Dogs are obviously not capable of solving even a simple math problem, but they excel when it comes to evaluating sensory input. What might fluster humans is second nature to dogs, and vice versa. Because of their superior senses, the dog world is in some ways much more vibrant than ours. And unlike us, dogs live very much in the present. They focus primarily on the here and now.

*Manipulating the rewards in
your dog's life will bring you
success in the training game.*

Your dog investigates everything in her universe and assesses the feed-back from each stimulus. Behaviors followed by good consequences are much more likely to be repeated in the future.

Dogs make thoughtful associations between their behavior and environmental cues and consequences. Moreover, dogs learn quickly by making new associations at an amazing rate. Thus, by providing appropriate feedback, owners can quickly and easily teach their dogs what they think is right. By manipulating the things your dog wants (food toys, attention, and life rewards) you can control the consequences of your dog's actions, and you can teach her to do just about anything you want. By the same token, inappropriate feedback will teach your dog to do things you don't want her to. For example, responding to your dog when she whines or jumps up on you will teach her that doing so is a good way to get your attention. So simply be sure your dog gets what *she* wants only when she does what *you* want.

Housetraining

Housetraining can be a breeze if you use dog-friendly methods. It is as simple as preventing mistakes (using on-leash supervision and confinement) and rewarding your dog for eliminating in the right spot (indoors on pads, paper, or litter; or outdoors).

Being a good doggy time manager is what housetraining is all about— making sure that your dog is in the right place at the right time. Mistakes happen because the dog is either in the right place at the wrong time or in the wrong place at the right time. If, for example, you take your dog for a walk to relieve himself when he doesn't need to go, he will probably need to go when he gets back inside! This is an example of being in the right place (outside) at the wrong time (when he doesn't need to go). Once the dog gets back inside, you have an example of being in the wrong place (inside) at the right time (when he needs to go).

During housetraining, your dog needs to be taken to his doggy toilet (the right place) when he needs to eliminate (the right time), and he

Every time your puppy gets it right and is rewarded for it, getting it right is reinforced. So set up your pup to get it right!

needs to be rewarded for going. All you have to do is make sure you don't give him the opportunity to make any mistakes in the wrong spot, and pretty soon your dog will have developed a strong habit and desire to eliminate in a particular area—his doggy toilet. Developing this strong habit is the essence of housetraining.

Dogs usually need a trip to the doggy toilet thirty to ninety minutes after eating a meal or drinking, so a well-planned feeding and watering schedule will help you determine when your dog will need to relieve himself. Your dog will also need to go after playing and when he wakes up. So you can be pretty sure that your dog will need to go to the bathroom when he wakes up, soon after eating and drinking, and after playing. This is especially true with puppies who haven't yet developed strong bladder and bowel muscles.

However, successful housetraining requires more accurately predicting when your dog needs to go. The best way to do so is to use confinement. Confining your dog to a small area, such as a crate, inhibits him from eliminating because most puppies and dogs naturally want to keep their sleeping areas clean. So your dog will need to eliminate when you release him from his crate and take him to his doggy toilet.

Don't fall into the trap of thinking that confining your dog is cruel. Using confinement in an educated manner is not unkind, especially considering how it accelerates housetraining (and chew-toy training) and therefore how quickly your dog can be trusted to spend his time in all safe areas of your home. We use confinement to help keep our children safe (for example, cribs), and we can likewise use it with our dogs.

Don't Kill with Kindness

One of the most common errors people make is allowing their dogs to be in a position to make mistakes because they feel guilty about using management tools to prevent them. Limiting your dog's freedom until he understands the house rules (where to eliminate, what to chew, etc.) is one of the kindest things you can do. This way, your dog will have a lifetime of freedom in your home, and you can be confident that he won't make mistakes.

Tools for Time Management

Supervision, food-stuffed chew toys, short-term and long-term confinement, and a food and water schedule are the five best tools to aid you in housetraining. Depending on your dog's age and level of training, as well as the particulars of your lifestyle, you may choose to use only some of these tools. However, the wise use of all five will help your dog avoid mistakes whether you are home or not. As a side benefit, using these tools is also a great way to prevent separation anxiety and avoid puppy nipping, inappropriate chewing, and greeting problems. These tools should all be used diligently until your dog understands the house rules, at which point he may enjoy as much freedom in your home as you feel is appropriate.

Supervision

Just as you would diligently supervise a young child in your home, so should you diligently supervise a puppy or "adult dog in housetraining."

Until he is housetrained, your dog should be supervised whenever he spends time in the home (unless he is in one of the two confinement areas listed below). You must be able to give him 100 percent of your attention. Taking your eyes off your dog for even a few moments is plenty of time for him to urinate, defecate, chew on the furniture (or worse), or chew on an electrical cord or other hazardous object.

Keeping your puppy or new adult dog on leash during these supervised times out of his confinement areas is a great idea until he is housetrained and chew-toy trained. The leash will remind you to watch him like a hawk. It is also a good idea to bring him into areas of the home outside of his confinement area only when you know that he has an empty bladder and bowel (that is, after you have just seen him eliminate in his doggy toilet), or until he is housetrained.

Give your dog a chew toy, step on his leash, and settle down with a good book. In no time, your dog will have a habit of settling quietly at your side, even without a leash on. When necessary, take him to his doggy toilet and let him relieve himself.

For the first week, keep the leash connected to you. Either step on it to keep your dog by your side, hold it in your hand, or tie it to a stable object right next to you. Your pup can spend his time playing a game with you, chewing on a chew toy, or just resting.

As your puppy or dog starts to understand the rules, you can give him a little more access to the room you are in by tethering him to a stable object nearby or by letting him drag the leash behind him (but only at a very short distance away!). Eventually, he will be housetrained and chew-toy trained and will be able to enjoy time off leash in his home.

Short-Term Confinement

The primary function of short-term confinement is to predict the exact time of elimination. There are many side benefits, including preventing your dog from making mistakes in your home and teaching your dog to tolerate quiet time alone. In regard to its use for housetraining, your dog has a natural inhibition against soiling his sleeping area. If your puppy has been confined in his bed or crate or on leash by your side for thirty minutes or more, you can bet that he will promptly relieve himself when taken to his doggy toilet.

By taking your puppy or dog out often, you will have many opportunities to show him where the right place is to go, and you will teach him to build bladder and bowel muscle control gradually and therefore successfully. Short periods spent in his confinement area have the added benefits of getting your dog accustomed to being left alone (essential for preventing separation anxiety issues) and teaching what is appropriate to chew (the chew toys you leave with him).

When you are away from home for short periods, confine your dog to his short-term area—either a crate or a tie-down. When you are home, keep your dog in his short-term confinement area if you cannot devote 100 percent of your attention to him.

What's a Tie-Down?

A *tie-down* is sort of like a crate without walls. Using a leash, tie your dog to a stable object (such as a heavy piece of furniture or an eye hook in the wall),

Some owners prefer a simple tie-down, "a crate without walls."

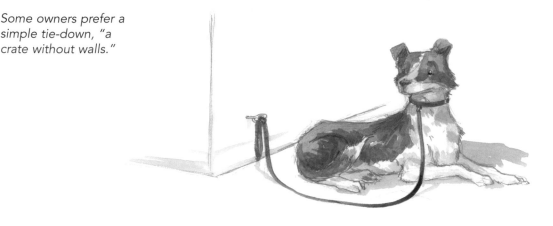

or simply step on the leash to keep your dog at your side. Just as with a crate, a tie-down is meant to inhibit your dog's elimination and keep him in a safe area so he can't chew inappropriate objects and otherwise get into trouble.

Get Your Dog Comfortable with His Crate

While it is true that dogs in the wild are considered den animals, that does not mean that your dog will necessarily take to his crate—if only for the fact that, unlike a den, a crate has a door that you close securely. You need to teach your dog to tolerate, and eventually enjoy, his personal space. There are two steps to this process:

1. Associating the crate with things your dog already likes (food and toys)

2. Gradually increasing the length of time that your dog spends in his crate

Be sure to put your dog in his crate only after you have seen him eliminate, so you are sure that his bladder and bowels are empty and there is very little chance of him soiling in this area.

Start by leaving the crate door open and tossing in a few treats. Your dog will eventually go in to investigate, especially if you plan the first few sessions during his mealtimes. When he moves confidently into the crate, offer him some extra-tasty, tiny treats for staying in there for an extra moment or two. You can gradually increase the time you have him wait in the crate for his treat from one second to two, three, four, five seconds, and so on. By repeating this process, your dog will start to want to go into the crate. Why? Because that's where all the good stuff is!

Now, when you put your dog in the crate, wait a few moments before giving him a treat. At this point, you might try giving him a food-stuffed chew toy. If you have already created a chew-toy habit in your dog, this process will be even easier because he will be occupied with his chew toy and hardly notice that he is confined.

It is advisable to feed your dog some of his meals in the crate. At first, feed from a bowl, but gradually work toward feeding from food-stuffed chew toys so that when he heads into the crate (which has become his dining room!), he is prepared to hang out and work at his toys to get his meal.

A good general rule is that you should confine your dog in his crate for only as long as you are willing to bet $500 (or whatever sum is important to you!) that he can hold it. And of course, never exceed a length of time that is reasonable and humane. Like any tool, the crate must be used thoughtfully and purposefully in order to be useful to you and pleasant for your dog. If introduced correctly, the crate can become a source of great comfort to your dog, as it is a place where he goes to rest, eat, and play with his food-stuffed toys.

Can My Puppy Sleep through the Night?

To help your puppy sleep as long as possible, take away his water three to four hours before you plan to put him to bed, unless your pup is not feeling well and your veterinarian advises otherwise. If you aren't willing to bet that your pup can hold it through the night, then you can leave him in a well-designed long-term confinement area, giving him access to a toilet so there will be no need for you to wake up to take him outside. Alternatively, you can leave him in his crate in your bedroom and set your alarm so that you can wake your pup and carry him to his toilet. This is wiser than allowing him to wake you by crying or barking. After he goes, bring him right back to his crate to go back to sleep; do not play with him, or you will teach him to wake you to play.

Daytime Crate Duration Guidelines

Here is a general guideline for the length of time a puppy can spend in a crate before getting a break to go to the bathroom. As a general rule, a puppy can hold it longer at night than during the day.

Puppy's age	Provide a break for your puppy
8–10 weeks	Approximately every 30–60 minutes
11–14 weeks	Approximately every 1–3 hours
15–17 weeks	Approximately every 3–4 hours
18+ weeks	Approximately every 4+ hours (6 hours maximum)

Long-Term Confinement

If your schedule does not permit you to be present to let your puppy or "adult dog in housetraining" out for frequent opportunities to eliminate, then you should leave him in a long-term confinement area. This area should provide your dog with everything he will need—chew toys, water or ice cubes, and a suitable indoor toilet. The indoor toilet is only necessary until your puppy has built sufficient bladder and bowel control and can be expected to hold it for several hours at a time. However, if you have a very small dog, you may want to have your dog use an indoor toilet permanently in addition to eliminating outdoors.

Long-term confinement options include:

✦ A bathroom gated off with a baby gate.

✦ An exercise pen.

✦ An exercise pen that includes a crate. In this case, the crate is the dog's bedroom and the dog's toilet is in the area sectioned off by the ex-pen.

✦ A crate connected to a doggy door that leads to a safely enclosed dog run. Your dog will essentially have a toilet and a bedroom. With this setup, your dog will all but housetrain himself!

If you leave an unhousetrained dog confined to a crate for a long period, he will be forced to soil his sleeping area. This is not only unkind, but it will also make it extremely difficult to housetrain him. So, for lengthy periods of confinement, either plan to have someone come in to give your dog a relief walk or leave your dog in an area that has a toilet if you can't offer him adequate relief walks from his crate and he is not yet capable of holding it for prolonged periods.

When spending time in his long-term confinement area, your dog can't make house-soiling (and chewing) mistakes in the rest of the house. So, rather than leave your puppy or dog to roam around your home and

An ideal and easy-to-construct long-term confinement area.

make mistakes (for which he will inevitably be punished later), it is much wiser simply to keep your dog in one safe area until he can be trusted to handle freedom in your home.

Yippee! You're Here!

When you get your pup from his sleeping area in the morning, don't encourage his excitement at your arrival. Doing so will only make him more likely to have an accident before you get him to his toilet. Instead, calmly walk in and immediately pick him up to take him to the area where you expect him to relieve himself. Then, of course, let him know how fantastic it is that he went in the right place.

Choosing a Doggy Toilet

One of the first things you need to do in housetraining is choose where you want your dog to eliminate. There are three basic options for your dog's toilet: outside on grass or concrete, inside on a doggy toilet, or both inside and outside. Having an adult dog who is trained to go inside on a doggy toilet in addition to outdoors can be very convenient and is often the choice for owners of small dogs.

Housetraining Puppies versus Adult Dogs

The only difference between housetraining a puppy and housetraining an adult dog is time. Pups generally take a little longer because of their limited bladder and bowel muscle control. Consequently, puppies need to go more frequently and therefore require more diligent time management and more frequent trips to their doggy toilet (at least once every hour or two for very young pups under 10 weeks of age).

Indoor Potty Training

If you have a young puppy and you can't be home to take him out as frequently as necessary during the day, then use a temporary indoor toilet. A very young puppy needs to go to the bathroom so often (just like a human baby) that it is inconvenient for most people to have to take him out often enough (especially if you live in a high-rise apartment). If your schedule permits, however, you can avoid using an indoor toilet simply by taking the pup outside as frequently as you think he needs to go.

Paper or Pad Training

If you choose to use papers or specially designed pads to train your pup, cover the *entire* floor of his long-term confinement area with paper or pads so that he can't make a mistake by going off of it. Don't assume that your pup will know to target a small area of paper or pad. Even if he does so at first, this doesn't necessarily indicate that it will remain a strong habit. It is best to set up your pup for success by covering the whole floor for at least a few days until you are confident that he has developed a strong preference for eliminating on your chosen surface. Every few days, remove a sheet or two until you are down to a small covered area. If he misses the paper or pad, then you have taken up too much too fast, and you should go back and cover more of the floor. Obviously, you will want to replace the paper or pads several times a day, so stock up!

Set Up Your Dog for Success

Your top priority when housetraining your dog is to do all you can to set him up to be successful. Every opportunity you give him to make a mistake sets him up to fail. So use a little tough love and be diligent about the wise use of all the management tools so that he has the best chance of being housetrained as fast as possible.

A Smooth Transition from Indoors to Outdoors

Ideally, it is a good idea to have an indoor doggy toilet that has the same surface as the one he will eventually use outside. Most people try to housetrain young puppies by teaching them to go on paper or pads and then outside on grass or concrete. But switching surfaces (from paper or pads to grass or concrete) when the dog is 3 to 4 months old means that housetraining is a two-step process: first teaching the dog to go on one surface inside and then on another surface outside. If you intend for your adult dog to have an outdoor toilet, bring a little bit of the great outdoors into your home. Get a roll of grass sod or a thin slab of concrete and place it in a large plastic litter box or a motor oil drip pan. If you choose to use grass turf or concrete in a litter pan, simply confine your pup to an area that is small enough that the pan takes up most of the area (aside from his bed). This arrangement may sound a little strange, but it will make house-training all the easier.

You will need to replace the grass or concrete at least once a week. Unless you want your dog to be litter-box trained in the future, you will use this indoor doggy toilet only until the puppy is old enough to control his bladder and bowel movements for longer periods in his crate.

If you must use a temporary indoor toilet in a long-term confinement area, be sure to use every opportunity (evenings and weekends) to get your pup to learn to hold it in his short-term area so that you can take him to the right spot outside to eliminate. This way, you are helping your pup strengthen his bladder and bowel muscles, and you can make an eas-ier transition to getting him to go outside quickly, consistently, and per-manently in the future.

A roll of turf is a marvelous innovation for a temporary indoor doggy toilet. It will speed up housetraining like you won't believe.

Quick Tips for Housetraining

✦ Give your dog every opportunity he needs to eliminate in the place you have chosen as his toilet.

✦ Praise and reward him lavishly when he goes on his doggy toilet.

✦ Give him zero opportunity to eliminate anywhere other than his designated doggy toilet.

Outdoor Potty Training

Teaching your dog to eliminate outdoors may require some patience if you expect him to eliminate on an unfamiliar surface such as concrete. This is especially true if you live in a city and your puppy or dog is not yet familiar with the sights, sounds, and smells, which can be overwhelming for some dogs.

When you take your dog to his outdoor doggy toilet, start by teaching him this new behavior at times when you are most sure he needs to eliminate. The best time is usually first thing in the morning.

Don't make the mistake of trying to walk your dog around the block to get him to go. Usually, this prolongs the process because your dog will get distracted, and some dogs who like to walk learn to hold it because they learn that the walk ends the moment they go. Instead, teach your dog to go to the bathroom right when you take him outside to a designated spot. Then the walk can be a reward for prompt elimination. On a cold and rainy night, you will be glad that you taught your dog to go quickly!

Walk back and forth in one area that's about 10 feet long, and wait about five minutes for him to go. If your dog doesn't go within five minutes, go back inside, keeping your dog on leash and on your lap (if possible). This is especially important with a puppy, whose bladder control is not yet very good, because you want to prevent a mistake. Sit down and read or watch television for ten to fifteen minutes before going back out to try again. This process usually takes no more than two or three attempts. Once your dog is rewarded with tasty, tiny treats and praise, he will start to understand what is expected when you head outside. Your dog is likely to go more and more promptly each time he is rewarded for doing so.

Perfect Aim

If you don't want your dog to use the whole yard as a toilet, you can train him to relieve himself in a specific area. Dogs are very particular about where they eliminate, so it is easy to teach a dog to go in a specific spot. Use posts and/or string to create a boundary. Take your dog on leash to this spot and reward him with a special treat for going there. In no time, he'll head straight for his special spot as you go out the door.

House-Soiling Mistakes
How to Get Your Dog Back on Track

If your adult dog is soiling in the house, the first thing to do is visit your veterinarian to make sure that the problem is not caused by a medical condition. If the vet says that everything is A-OK, then there are just a few steps to getting your dog back on the right housetraining track. When you can't supervise him, be sure to confine him to a long-term or short-term confinement area. When you can supervise him, have him near you on leash (and with a food-stuffed chew toy) so that you can prevent mistakes. When you take him outside and he relieves himself, give him three tiny, tasty treats for going in the right spot. In no time flat, you'll have a dog who hasn't been allowed to practice going in the wrong place and who sees the value in going in the right place.

Housetraining is as easy as 1, 2, 3. (1) Confine your dog to prevent mistakes and (2) to predict when he needs to go so that you can (3) take your dog to the right place and reward him handsomely!

Keep Your Cool

Accidents will happen no matter how diligent you are. Whatever you do, don't get angry at your dog. If your dog makes a mistake in the house, yelling at him or otherwise punishing him will serve only to teach him two things: that you aren't so nice after all, and that you don't like to see him go to the bathroom. Your dog will think, "Obviously, my owner has some weird urination issues and wants me to do it in private." As a result, he will learn that the safest time to eliminate is when you aren't around, and you will find that he is highly unlikely to go when you are at the other end of the leash. Instead, he will find hidden spots, like behind the couch.

Remember, if your dog makes a mistake in the house, it tells you that he isn't housetrained after all. Either you failed to put him in the right

After being yelled at for going in the house, this dog is thinking that his owner has some hang-ups about urination.

As a result, he has learned not to go when the neurotic one is watching.

And so he is forced to hide to eliminate.

place when he needed to go or you neglected to confine him when you couldn't watch him.

If You Catch Him in the Act

If your dog eliminates in front of you in the house, quickly say "outside." Then scoop him up (if possible) and take him to his doggy toilet. Praise and reward him with a tasty little treat when he goes out there. Perhaps most important, let this incident serve as a reminder that you need to be more diligent about preventing mistakes.

Submissive or Excitement Urination

If your dog urinates when he greets you or others or when you yell at him, he is trying to appease you by saying in the way some dogs do, "Please don't hurt me; I'm submissive." Submissive urination is most frequently seen in dogs who lack confidence due to inadequate socialization and in dogs who have been subjected to physical or verbal corrections.

Immediately discontinue using any sort of verbal and physical punishments; they will only make matters worse. Your dog is urinating as an appeasement gesture. If you respond with a correction, your dog is likely to get even more nervous and urinate more. In addition, you will further damage your relationship with your dog.

The solution is to set your dog up to be successful when he greets people so that he isn't so worried. For a couple of days, toss a small handful of tiny treats on the ground when you approach your dog. This way, he'll be focused on the treats (and not on being concerned about you), and he'll start to associate your approach with great things (tasty treats). If he urinates on the first greeting, simply ignore him. Leave, come back, and greet him again. It is unlikely that he will urinate on the second or subsequent greetings, so you may further reward him for dry greetings by dropping more tiny treats on the floor.

After a few days, offer the treat from your hand. Then use the treats to teach your dog to sit to greet by waiting for him to do so, marking the behavior with a click or "yes," and offering the treat. You can also lure your dog to sit by holding a treat over his head as you approach. Refrain from saying "sit," because he doesn't yet know what is expected, and saying "sit" will not necessarily get him to do so. Commanding him to sit may also cause him worry, which could cause him to urinate. Repeat these silent greetings many times over the course of a few days.

After a few more days have passed, you can approach and calmly ask your dog to sit as you expect him to (since he has practiced this behavior for days) or use the food to lure him to do so. At this point, it is likely that he has come to view your approach, your hand movements, and now your request to sit as signals that he is about to get something great from you. In this state of mind, he is unlikely to urinate.

Don't yell at or hit your dog if he makes a mistake in the house; it will only make matters worse. Instead, reprimand yourself!

Work on socializing a submissive dog to lots of people so that he gets a boost in self-confidence. You might consider taking him to a dog-training class or dog park, where he is sure to meet lots of dog-friendly people, or invite some friends over. (See Chapter 4 for more on socialization.)

Housetraining Mistakes to Be Spiteful?

If you think your dog has made a housetraining mistake to be spiteful (maybe you think he is upset with you for leaving him all day?), think again. As wonderfully gifted as dogs can be (consider guide dogs for the blind and bomb-detection dogs), a dog is not capable of thinking of holding and then specifically placing his urine or feces as a way of punishing you. It is more likely that a housetraining mistake was made because the dog:

✦ Was not truly housetrained to begin with

✦ Was not feeling well

✦ Has been punished for elimination and so waited to go until you (the big, bad punisher) were not there to punish him

✦ Was stressed (maybe due to you leaving), which caused him to have to relieve himself

The Three Steps to Successful Housetraining

Remember, the wise use of supervision and confinement when you can't supervise your dog enables you to:

1. Make sure that your dog is never in the wrong place at the right time. This ensures that your dog doesn't make any mistakes, because each mistake sets the precedent for more to follow.

2. Make sure that your dog is in the right place at the right time when he needs to go to the bathroom.

3. Predict when your dog needs to go so that you can take your dog to his doggy toilet at the appropriate time and reward him for going. This is the real secret of successful housetraining.

4 Improve Your Dog's Social Life

can't think of a more important quality in a pet dog than to be friendly to people, especially to children. Consequently, there are no more pressing items on your dog's training agenda than socialization and habituation. Socialization and habituation make your dog fit to be a great companion. Well-socialized dogs develop confidence and do not become overly dependent on their owners. They are better equipped to calmly handle a variety of situations around people or when left at home alone. Because friendly dogs are a pleasure to be around, owners enjoy spending time playing with and training them. In turn, the dogs are much less likely to chew, bark excessively, or soil in the house. Obviously, a well-socialized dog has no need to hide or bite. And well-socialized dogs are certainly more likely to live longer, happier, healthier, and more enriched lives.

What Are Socialization and Habituation?

Socialization is the process that makes your dog friendly with animals and, even more important, with people. Sure, it would be a severe inconvenience if your dog were unfriendly to other dogs, especially if you must walk your dog on the street and pass other dogs every day. But it would be a more pressing and constant worry if your dog were unfriendly to people, and it would be a disaster if your dog were not friendly to family members.

The Benefits of Good Social Skills

A well-socialized dog is a friend to all, and she'll be a welcome guest. Yes, you want your dog to be a party animal! Most behavior problems, including aggression, fear, housesoiling, not coming when called, separation anxiety, chewing, and barking, stem from poor socialization.

First, you should socialize the dog to your family, but this step alone is not sufficient, no matter what size your dog. Many owners of superfriendly family dogs experience a rude awakening when the dog snaps at a visiting child, a stranger in the dog park, or the veterinarian. It's great that the dog likes Mom, Dad, the two kids, and a couple of family friends, since these are the people your dog will spend most of her time with. But socialization means teaching your dog to be friendly and accepting of *all* people you introduce to her, especially unfamiliar children and men, as these two groups of people are the most likely to be bitten by a dog. It is not sufficient to teach your dog just to get along with her usual social

*Take your dog on frequent trips down
the socialization roadway.*

circle. There is always the chance that an unfamiliar child or veterinary technician will handle your dog, and you want her to be prepared for the encounter.

Habituation is the process of familiarizing your dog with stimuli (sights, sounds, smells, and experiences) so that she becomes comfortable with them. The more stimuli your dog is comfortable with, the less likely she is to suffer from fear or anxiety and to develop related behavior problems.

Be aware that socialization and habituation are ongoing processes. Your dog must continue to meet unfamiliar people and animals and be exposed to new sights, sounds, smells, and experiences throughout her life if you wish for her to continue to be a friendly dog.

Puppy Socialization and Habituation

Although you can obedience-train a dog at any age, a sound temperament is something that should be nurtured and improved upon early in life. If you delay this process, you can still socialize your adolescent or adult dog, but it will be much more time-consuming, and you could be playing catch-up for years to come.

Watchdogs Are Friendly, Too!

Some people resist socializing their dogs to strangers because they want their dogs to be protective. Your dog's innate ability to choose between friend and foe might be pretty accurate, but eventually she may make a mistake. It's much smarter to socialize your dog first so that she is confident and secure in the company of all people. Then, if you choose, train your dog to bark or growl on cue as a protective ruse.

The concept of early socialization and puppy training was rediscovered and popularized by dogs' best friend, English veterinarian and behaviorist Dr. Ian Dunbar. No other training innovation has had such a dramatic influence on the lives of pet dogs and their owners around the world than this one. Early socialization is the best way to create your perfect companion and to avoid behavior and temperament problems.

Certainly, puppy-training concepts are not new. In fact, they're so old that they're new again! Both dog and horse texts from the 1800s talk about early training and gentling procedures, but many of these concepts were lost to the world of dog and horse trainers for the greater part of the twentieth century. However, the word has spread, and puppy socialization and training are at the forefront of modern dog lovers' agendas. In fact, you can find puppy playgroups, puppy-training classes, and adult dog socialization groups in just about every town and city. Thanks to Dr. Dunbar and others like him, the socialization revolution has been very successful!

A Puppy's Development

An understanding of the developmental stages a puppy goes through in the first few months of her life is valuable whether you are working with a young pup or an adult dog. In either case, it's important to consider that these early weeks are the foundation for her behavior for a lifetime.

Birth to 21 days: During this period, the puppy has an extremely limited mental capacity and reacts only to her needs for warmth, food, and sleep. At the end of this period, the pup's eyes begin to open, and as a result the pup begins to respond to movement and sounds.

21st to 28th day: During this time, the puppy's brain and nervous system begin to develop rapidly. At this stage, the pup has a greater sense of awareness and is strongly affected by conditions and experiences.

5th to 7th week: At this stage, the puppy is likely to begin to explore her surroundings and develop a greater social awareness of both her litter-mates and any people she is exposed to (especially in regard to recognizing voices). A social order within the litter starts to establish itself; it is most obvious at feeding times, when some pups fight confidently for food (the pups begin biting), while others wait passively. The pups' mother begins weaning them and teaching them basic manners, especially in regard to taking food gently from her. If they are too rough, she will get up to walk away.

8th to 12th week: The pup's ability to learn is at full capacity by this point. It is crucial to take advantage of this period so that you can make the most of your pup's ability to learn so much in such a short time. Your pup's bladder and bowel muscles are starting to develop, and some pups at this age can sleep through the night.

13th to 16th week: During this period, the puppy is likely to begin asserting herself and displaying greater independence, much like a toddler. It is especially important to control resources (food, toys, attention, and the environment) so that they are useful as tools to teach your pup to behave politely, especially in regard to curbing nipping.

17th to 24th week: At this stage, the puppy is much like a 13-year-old child. The pup is likely to demonstrate greater independence and may seem to be challenging you every step of the way. She is coping with the pain of teething as well as the hormonal changes that result from moving toward sexual maturity.

25th to 72nd week: During this period of young adulthood, the pup is likely to be full of energy and exuberance. It is crucial that you continue to help her focus that energy in positive ways and improve her understanding of how you want her to behave so that she can mature into the dog of your dreams!

Getting Used to Sounds

It is vital to expose very young pups to a variety of noises, especially during the first few weeks of life, as their ears are opening. This exposure enables developing pups to become accustomed to loud and potentially scary noises in a gradual fashion. Getting accustomed to many different sounds is a key ingredient in creating a dog who gets to experience and enjoy lots of social situations throughout her life.

When familiarizing a puppy with various sounds, perhaps the most important precaution you can take is to ensure that the puppy has been raised indoors—not in a barn, not in a kennel, but inside a home, which is where you will want her to be with you for her whole life. Ideally, she will be situated in an area where she has exposure to the comings and goings of the household. This

Turn on the TV to help your pup get used to lots of noises, and you might find that you have the same favorite shows!

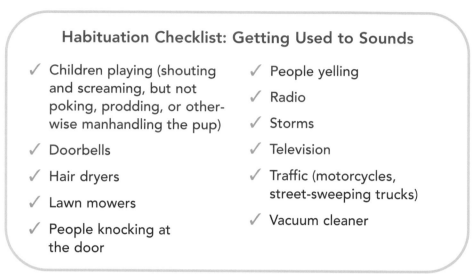

Habituation Checklist: Getting Used to Sounds

✓ Children playing (shouting and screaming, but not poking, prodding, or otherwise manhandling the pup)

✓ Doorbells

✓ Hair dryers

✓ Lawn mowers

✓ People knocking at the door

✓ People yelling

✓ Radio

✓ Storms

✓ Television

✓ Traffic (motorcycles, street-sweeping trucks)

✓ Vacuum cleaner

precaution is especially important with sound-sensitive breeds, such as guarding breeds. If you have done your homework and have chosen a pup who has been raised inside a home or in a shelter that provides an enriching environment, then you know she is already off to a good start on her journey down the socialization highway! But don't fret if you are adopting a puppy or an adult dog and don't know her background. Simply do your best to expose her to a host of normal, everyday noises in her new home. So no tiptoeing around this little girl. Turn up the radio, open the windows, and start vacuuming!

Getting Used to Surfaces

Some dogs are very sensitive to particular surfaces and will do all they can to avoid walking across them. You can prevent such issues by gradually exposing your pup to various surfaces right away. Praise, food, and toys can be useful motivators and rewards when teaching your dog to be comfortable on varied surfaces.

Habituation Checklist: Getting Used to Surfaces

✓ Ceramic tile   ✓ Mud

✓ Grass   ✓ Stairs

✓ Gravel   ✓ Wood flooring

✓ Ice   ✓ Other slippery surfaces

Make Your Dog a Social Climber

Climbing the social ladder can be tough for people, but you can have a whole lot of fun helping your dog climb her social ladder. Let her experience as many things as possible in a rewarding setting so that she becomes a confident and well-adjusted member of your family. The earlier you start, the better. By 16 weeks, your puppy's view of the world and her place in it has already become well established, but it is never too late for your dog to become better equipped socially.

Getting to Know People

To keep up with her developmental timetable, your puppy needs to be well on her way in regard to socialization with people by the time she is 4 months old. As a general rule, your pup needs to have met at least fifty different people in a positive setting. Fifty people by 4 months old? Actually, it's easy. All you have to do is invite people to your home and have a few puppy parties!

Some people have told me that this is an unrealistic demand to make of a new puppy owner. But again, nothing is more important for a pet dog than to be well socialized and friendly. And there is no better time to lay the foundation than in early puppyhood. Investing time and energy in this process early on will save you a whole lot of time and energy (and probably grief) later on. Anyway, socializing your puppy is fun! Put the word out to your friends that they can come and play with your new dog, and chances are you'll have to throw a few little parties a week to accommodate them all! If you can find a puppy class in your area, all the better.

Helping Your Pup Gain Confidence

If your puppy or dog shows signs of stress when exposed to something, let her gain confidence gradually in well-planned training sessions. Be prepared with plenty of high-level reinforcers (your dog's favorite treats and toys), which you can offer while she is at a safe distance from the thing she is scared of and gradually make closer contact. Don't try to force the situation or accidentally encourage the fearful reaction by saying something like "Poor puppy!" This well-intentioned attention is likely to make the problem worse.

Puppy Parties

If you want a dog who is friendly with people and other animals, you must begin socializing in puppyhood and maintain socialization throughout the dog's life. There is no better way to introduce your dog to numerous people in pleasant and rewarding settings than to host puppy parties in your home or at a local training school or veterinary practice.

Initially, invite close family and friends, and teach them all to use tiny bits of food (you can use your dog's normal meals or special treats) to

teach your dog to come,
sit, and lie down. Not only
will your friends train your
dog for you, but your dog
also will learn to love people.
Be sure to invite women and
men, as well as children, a few
at a time.

Once the puppy is thor-
oughly at ease with all sorts of
people, it's time for a little fri-
volity. Have costume parties where everybody
wears a hat, carries something unusual, and adopts silly
mannerisms. This might sound a little ridiculous, but it's
for a serious reason. Basically, after a series of puppy parties
like these, little in the real world will really scare your dog. For example,
if a child who has dressed up for Halloween as a frog hops by your dog and
taps her on the head with a wand, your pup will think, "Been there, done
that!" and wag her tail happily.

Puppy parties are the best way to improve your dog's social life—and yours, too!

If it is unrealistic for you to host a puppy party in your home, all you
have to do is contact a local trainer or veterinarian, who may already host
their own weekly puppy parties. If not, suggest that they do!

Get your dog used to the strange things people do, too, like staring
and manhandling. Sadly, not everyone is respectful of a dog's limits, and
it's likely that at some point someone will touch your dog a little more
roughly than is appropriate. So get your dog used to this now when she is

a puppy. In fact, if you do things right, you will have a dog who not only tolerates, but *enjoys* just about any sort of handling!

Start by having family members hand-feed while they stare at and touch the pup. Touch her very gently at first. Gradually, increase the force of your handling. At the same time, you might want to increase the value of the rewards. Work up to being able to be only as rough as a typical child might be if left unsupervised. Not that any young child should be left unsupervised with a dog, but if it happens by accident, you want a dog who is as prepared as possible. After practicing for a week or so, invite a friend over and have her hand-feed your dog while she gently touches the dog and you handle the dog a little more roughly. Eventually, you should have a dog who is comfortable with just about anyone handling her in just about any way (within reason, of course).

Don't Keep Your Puppy a Secret!

Remember, your puppy needs to meet fifty people before she is 4 months old. Make a point to invite your neighbors and their children over to meet your puppy. Neighborhood children are less likely to taunt or be afraid of a dog they get to know as a puppy. And when your dog is old enough to go outside, walk her on a different route at least once a day so she meets lots of unfamiliar people.

Socialization Checklist: Getting to Know People

✓ Family

✓ Friends

✓ Visitors (strangers)

✓ Children

✓ Elderly people

✓ Joggers

✓ Mail carriers and delivery people

✓ People carrying things (baseball bats, bags, umbrellas)

✓ People in costumes

✓ People in the park

✓ People in the street

✓ People in uniform

✓ People in wheelchairs

✓ People of different ethnicities

✓ People on bicycles, skateboards, and inline skates

✓ People wearing hats

✓ People wearing sunglasses

✓ People who move quickly

✓ People who move slowly

✓ People with facial hair

✓ People using canes and walkers

Getting to Know Animals

Some socialization to animals will have to wait until the pup is old enough to go to a puppy-training class. Because the pup may have been in virtual social isolation (at least to dogs) since coming into your home, socializing your puppy to other appropriate dogs now becomes a major priority. Once you have enrolled her in puppy class, your pup will have lots of opportunities to meet other pups. Remember, although it's important, it's not sufficient that your dog becomes friendly with just a small circle of canine friends. She must learn how to greet unfamiliar dogs as well.

Playing with another dog can be great exercise for your dog, both mentally and physically. Set up doggy play dates with friends and people from dog-training class. You can also use this time to practice having your dog greet people nicely by sitting.

When socializing with other dogs, it's important to choose playmates carefully and monitor their interactions closely. Initially, let your dog play with pups of a similar age; then you can plan interactions with adult dogs who have good social skills and temperaments. While some dog parks can be a great experience for some dogs, they are generally not recommended as a starting point for socialization, as they can be overwhelming due to the constant influx of new dogs.

If you want to socialize your puppy to the resident cat, you have already done the right thing by starting early. It is generally much easier and safer for an adult cat and a young puppy to work things out than an adult dog and a young kitten. Have your pup on leash and give her a food-stuffed toy so that she is prevented from developing a habit of chasing the cat and instead learns to hang out calmly and play with her toys while the cat is in the room.

Cats and dogs can become the best of friends. But it helps to introduce them when the dog is a youngster.

Depending on where you live, you may or may not want to socialize your dog to horses and livestock and to teach her not to chase or

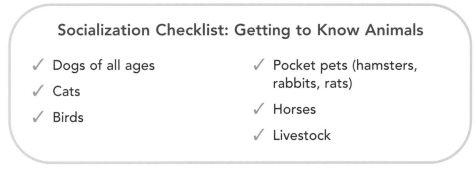

Socialization Checklist: Getting to Know Animals

✓ Dogs of all ages

✓ Cats

✓ Birds

✓ Pocket pets (hamsters, rabbits, rats)

✓ Horses

✓ Livestock

otherwise harass livestock or wild animals. Simply keep her on leash to prevent problems, and teach her to pay attention to you when you ask her to sit, lie down, and come when called (even around other animals). This training is covered in Chapter 7.

Getting to Know Places

You don't want an adult dog whose fun and freedom are limited because she feels uncomfortable in strange places. So make it a point to take your young puppy or new adult dog anywhere and everywhere with you. Without a doubt, the single most effective and enjoyable socialization procedure is walking (or carrying) your pup on different routes on a regular basis. There is simply no other activity that will prepare your pup for her life ahead in the same way.

Puppy Class

Again, one of the most important places to take your pup is to puppy class. This is perhaps one of the most exciting things you can do with your young pup. You both will learn a lot and have the time of your life. For many owners, puppy school moments are some of the most cherished

Puppy class is the best night out for you and your dog!

memories of spending time with their young dogs, as they are the foundation of learning how to communicate and bond with their canine companions. Don't miss out on this wonderful opportunities. Anyway, you wouldn't want to neglect your puppy's education, would you?

In puppy class, your pup will have ample opportunities to socialize with a variety of dogs and their owners. Apart from the fun aspect, the off-leash play sessions in puppy classes are essential for your puppy to learn bite inhibition and develop a soft mouth (see Chapter 5 for more on teaching your pup not to bite). Puppy class also provides a convenient opportunity for you to ask for professional advice on any pressing or potential puppy problems. To find a puppy class in your area, call the Association of Pet Dog Trainers at 800-PET-DOGS or go to www.apdt.com.

Socialization Checklist: Getting to Know Places

- ✓ Beaches
- ✓ Cars
- ✓ Crowded areas
- ✓ Dog-friendly shops
- ✓ Dog-training school
- ✓ Elevators and escalators
- ✓ Friends' homes

- ✓ Frequent walks
- ✓ Gas stations
- ✓ Grooming salon
- ✓ Parks
- ✓ Pet stores
- ✓ Public transport
- ✓ Veterinarian

The Social Small Dog

One of the many benefits of having a very small dog is how easy it is to get her from place to place by carrying her rather than having her walk by your side. But be sure your small dog has adequate social experiences in a position other than in your arms. If you don't, she may learn to be comfortable with things when in your arms but not when on the ground, since dogs are very specific learners.

Being overly protective can cause Small Dog Syndrome. Help your small dog gain life-long confidence by giving her a chance to encounter new experiences and challenges.

Adult Dog Socialization

If you're bringing a new adult dog into your home, your major concern is to check out how well socialized the dog is and to strengthen any weak spots.

For example, if you find that this dog is a bit uncomfortable with men in hats, then you must make a concerted effort to help your new dog learn to love men wearing hats. Invite one or two friends at a time to meet your new dog. Ask them to bring hats, but not to wear them. Have your dog on leash and ask everyone to take a seat. Have one friend (without his hat on) hand-feed the dog her dinner. When your dog is comfortable, have your friend place the hat on the floor or his lap and feed the dog. Then ask him to casually put on the hat and feed the dog. Make an effort to invite over as many of your male friends as possible, one or two at a time, to follow this procedure. Pretty soon your dog will be searching out men wearing hats because she will have learned that they are a generous bunch.

It's sad to see a dog who is afraid of people.

For a brush-up, read and follow the socialization exercises outlined in the puppy section.

Socializing an Adult Dog from a Shelter

Few things are more rewarding than giving a loving home to an adult dog from a shelter. However, keep in mind that, as with puppies, you might experience a couple of weeks of a honeymoon. As your dog becomes more comfortable in her new home, her true personality will shine through. Be especially careful to take things slowly so as not to push your dog too far too fast in regard to exposure to potentially new and frightening experiences.

Problems Caused by Failure to Socialize

Socializing a dog is so easy and so much fun that a lot of people fail to take it seriously. However, without adequate socialization and habituation, your dog may face situations she is not prepared to deal with. When a dog isn't comfortable, she is likely to react in one of two ways: by fighting or by running away. This is called the fight or flight instinct. As a result, she may develop three of the most serious and hard-to-resolve problems: biting, fighting, and barking.

Maintaining Socialization

Socialization is ongoing for the rest of your dog's life. Your dog may have gone to a puppy class (yippee!), and a lucky dog is walked on a fun, social route each day. But while this dog has met a number of people and a number of dogs, it is also likely that she will meet those same familiar faces each and every day. To keep your dog socialized, she must continue to meet new dogs and new people. The three best ways to do so are by

Make sure you socialize your dog to people and teach her how to greet visitors properly.

- ✦ Walking a different route each day
- ✦ Having small parties in your home
- ✦ Attending as many fun dog-training classes as possible

Doggy Dates

Set up as many safe, off-leash play sessions as possible so that your dog can make friends. This is one of the best ways to maintain your dog's socialization to other dogs. A good training school will offer a variety of weekly play dates for puppies and adult dogs.

5

Gentling and Handling

A great pet dog instills in his family the confidence that they or anyone else can easily handle and examine all parts of his body, take food and toys away from him, and play with him without fear of getting hurt. Practicing consistent gentling and handling exercises throughout your dog's lifetime, starting when you first bring him home, is the best way to prevent problems, such as a dog who squiggles and squirms or, worse, growls or bites when you try to groom, medicate, or otherwise care for or play with him, or when you go near his food bowl or reach to take a toy from him. Teaching your dog to accept handling willingly and happily is a top priority. Don't wait until your dog cuts his foot to find out that he doesn't like having his feet touched, or until he growls at a visiting child who approaches his food bowl to find out that he guards his food and toys.

Handling Exercises

Mealtimes Are Playtime!

As with all training, the more frequently you practice handling and the more fun and rewarding the exercises are, the more likely the exercises are to be successful. Therefore, practicing training exercises during your dog's mealtimes is a great idea. You can practice body handling as well as basic manners. He'll learn to associate being handled with something he already loves—his food. Also, since feeding your dog is part of your daily routine, practicing at mealtimes is a good reminder for you to maintain his skills by consistent repetition. Remember, the more you practice mealtime handling exercises, the more confident you can be that you will prevent problems later.

Consistently allowing your dog to eat his food alone may cause him to guard his food. Teach your dog to appreciate people being near his food bowl by making mealtimes a social experience.

Whenever possible and appropriate, include family members and friends in mealtime training exercises to teach your dog to appreciate people being near him when he eats his meals.

Play Doctor

This training exercise, where you "play doctor" with your dog, will effectively teach him to become comfortable with being handled. In a quiet area of your home, have your dog on leash. Start by gently touching an area of his body that you think he isn't likely to mind (usually around his back) for just one second, and then give him a piece of food. Repeat this process a few times and then move on to another part of his body. Many dogs are most sensitive around the head and feet, so handle these areas last so that your dog is clearly focused on the task at hand—allowing a brief touch for a bit of food. When he seems completely comfortable with a one-second touch on a particular body part, increase to two seconds before giving a piece of food. Your goal is to gradually increase the duration of each touch.

It's very important to go slowly. If you go too fast, you may miss subtle cues that your dog isn't enjoying being touched in a certain area.

Signs You're Moving Too Fast

If your dog does any of the following things excessively, you might be moving too quickly:

- Avoids eye contact with you
- Changes his ear placement
- Flinches
- Licks his lips more than normal
- Tries to pull away
- Turns his head away
- Yawns

In that case, take a step or two backward. If you are touching for five seconds, for example, go back to one or two seconds and consider upping the payoff for your dog. Maybe at this stage in the training game, your dog requires a tasty treat instead of a piece of dry food in exchange for you holding his paw.

Don't forget to gently examine your dog's mouth, take a look inside his ears, and check between his toes. For each new area you touch, offer a tasty bit of food. Be especially generous when you touch areas that your dog is more sensitive about: often the feet and around the head. If your dog is squirmy, you can tie him to something stable or have someone hold him at the beginning so that you have both hands free to pet and reward promptly.

Repeat this process with your dog's grooming tools. Start with one stroke of the brush, and then offer a piece of food. Now try two strokes and then a piece of food. Pick up one foot, lay nail clippers against it, and offer a bit of food. Then look into one of his ears and offer a piece of food. Don't rush things. Take time to make sure that your dog enjoys minimal examining before you actually clip a nail or clean his ear.

For the sake of both of your enjoyment, invite your dog over for a belly rub at least once a day. This is a great way to show him how enjoyable being handled can be. While rubbing him in a spot he likes very much, you can also gently handle his ears, feet, and other body parts.

A tummy rub and a treat will teach any puppy to love handling.

Handling Checklist: Getting Used to Handling

✓ Apply medications to your dog's skin or in his eyes or ears.

✓ Groom or bathe your dog.

✓ Inspect your dog's fur.

✓ Look inside your dog's ears and eyes.

✓ Look inside your dog's mouth.

✓ Take things from your dog's mouth.

✓ Touch your dog's back.

✓ Touch your dog's collar.

✓ Touch your dog's head.

✓ Touch your dog's paws.

✓ Touch your dog's rear end.

✓ Touch your dog's tummy.

You Look Marvelous!

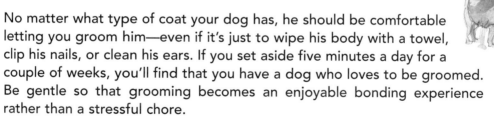

No matter what type of coat your dog has, he should be comfortable letting you groom him—even if it's just to wipe his body with a towel, clip his nails, or clean his ears. If you set aside five minutes a day for a couple of weeks, you'll find that you have a dog who loves to be groomed. Be gentle so that grooming becomes an enjoyable bonding experience rather than a stressful chore.

Sharing Exercises

Much like us, dogs are likely to protect those things that they find valuable. While it is normal and natural for dogs to gather and guard food, bones, toys, and other resources, this instinct can get a pet dog into a whole lot of trouble. It is obviously not appropriate for a dog to growl or snap when someone tries to take something from him. You can help your

> ## Resources Your Dog Might Consider Protecting
>
> ✓ Food
>
> ✓ Locations (such as a bed or couch)
>
> ✓ People
>
> ✓ Toys

dog avoid potential problems by showing him how rewarding it is to relinquish resources at your request.

Mealtime Handling

The food bowl is one of the resources a dog is most likely to guard. To prevent food bowl guarding, set aside at least a few minutes every day to participate in your dog's mealtimes. Your goal is to have a dog who is comfortable with people being near him while he eats (you should be able to walk close by, touch him, and put your hands in the bowl while he eats), and who is comfortable with you taking his bowl away.

Don't just set your dog's food down and walk away. Hang around while he eats. Touch him and talk to him. Every once in a while, particularly when you touch him, put a tasty treat in his bowl and show him how rewarding it is to have humans around his bowl.

Sit next to your dog and hold his bowl in your hand or lap. Hand-feed him

Mine! All mine! (This could be a problem. . . .)

a few bits of his meal at a time as you gently touch a part of his body. Now put the bowl on the ground next to you, place your hand with a few bits of food in the empty bowl, and let your dog eat the food from your hand. Then place the empty bowl on the ground, drop in a few bits of food, and reach toward the bowl to drop in a few more bits—and maybe even a special treat that you know your dog likes better than his normal meal. This way, he will start to understand that having you (and eventually other people) near him makes his meals appear and sometimes be even better than normal.

Practice getting up and walking a few feet away and then back to the bowl so that you can reach down, take it away, and offer a bit of food from the other hand, or simply drop a bit of food or a tasty treat into

the bowl and give it back to your dog. In both cases, your dog is learning that your approaching (and even taking away) the bowl is a good thing.

When possible and appropriate, include as many family members and friends in these exercises as possible. Be sure that children are always supervised around your dog, especially near the food bowl. If your adult dog is exhibiting signs of guarding (becoming tense, growling, or snapping when people come near the bowl), consult a dog-friendly trainer who can work with you in person to resolve this issue safely.

Mealtimes are a terrific opportunity to teach your dog to love having people near his food bowl and to prevent resource guarding.

Play the Trading Game

Regardless of how much he wants something, your dog must learn that if you or any other person reaches to take something away from him, he must relinquish it without a fuss. It is usually best to start this trading game with something that is of lower value to him, not his favorite toy. Simply offer him a toy and let him play with it for a moment or two. Then reach to take the toy as you say "thank you!" and offer a very tasty bit of food. Numerous repe-

Teach your dog to enjoy exchanging valued possessions.

titions of this game throughout the day are a surefire way to have your dog begging you to take away his toys. After a few three- to five-minute practice sessions, let him play with the toy (and get more engrossed in it) for a bit longer before you take it away and offer a treat.

Gradually introduce new toys to play the trading game with, working up to his favorites. When you play with objects you know your dog is more interested in, use food rewards that are more valuable. That is, with a toy of little interest, you can use a piece of your dog's dry food. But when trading for his favorite toy, offer a favorite treat.

When you feel confident that your dog is happily relinquishing toys, you can start to teach him to respond to the words "thank you" without the signal of your hand showing the food. Just say the word and wait until your dog looks for your hand, mark the behavior of looking away from the object with a click or by saying "yes," and then give the reward.

Gotcha!

In an emergency, you may need to grab your dog to get a hold of him, and a tragedy could result if your dog doesn't allow you to do so. Teach your dog to accept being grabbed by teaching him that it is a rewarding experience. Many times throughout the day, reach down to grab your dog's collar, say "Gotcha!" and at the same time give him a treat. In no time at all, your dog will love being grabbed.

Many dogs learn to avoid letting people grab their collar because they think it means the end of play or they are in trouble. Teach your dog to love being grabbed by practicing the Gotcha! exercises many times each day. Pretty soon he'll be begging to be grabbed!

Preventing Nipping in Play

Puppies in a litter spend a lot of their time nipping at each other, so it is no surprise that your pup may think this sort of normal dog play is all right with you. But, just as your puppy must learn to inhibit his bites with his canine playmates (if he hurts his friends, they won't want to play anymore), so must he learn to inhibit the use of his mouth with humans. In fact, learning to inhibit his formidable weapon is one of the most important lessons your dog will learn.

Surprisingly and luckily, the more your puppy bites you when he is very young, the better his bite inhibition is likely to be as an adult. Each time your pup bites is an opportunity to remind him how sensitive human skin is. On the other hand, a puppy who never bites humans can't learn how sensitive human skin is and how careful he must be.

With this is mind, don't attempt to tell your puppy to stop biting by yelling at him, grabbing his muzzle, or otherwise hurting him. Doing so may quickly stop the biting (for the moment) by scaring him. But imagine that one day your dog does bite someone, maybe because that person accidentally stepped on his paw. If this happens, it is essential that your dog cause as little harm as possible. You want a dog with superb bite inhibition. So the first thing to teach your pup is that human flesh is very sensitive, much more so than his littermates' skin. Your puppy should think about how careful he has to be when play-mouthing with you. Then you can work on curbing mouthing altogether.

Don't try this at home! Your dog can be trained to give on request.

Start by playing with your puppy only when he has a leash on. If you play with your puppy when he is off leash and he nips you, you have no way to gain control of the situation unless you grab for your pup. This will most likely get him even more riled up (most pups love to be chased), and it may teach him to avoid you (if you reprimand him when you do catch him) and potentially teach him to avoid being grabbed—something you will regret if your dog ever gets off leash on the street by accident.

Keeping the dog on leash is especially prudent for children, who can play with a puppy when supervised. This is the perfect way to prevent nipping, jumping, and overly exuberant play. You can also tether the pup to a stable object so that the child can get up and walk away without the pup being able to practice chasing and nipping.

When your puppy goes to bite you, respond with a time-out by standing up (if you are in his long-term confinement area), using his leash to hold him gently at arm's length, or stepping on the leash so he can't move

Until your dog learns to play calmly with children, practice supervised play/training sessions with your dog on a leash so he remains stationed and calm.

about and play. Wait a few moments, and then try playing again. The force of your pup's next nibble should come down a bit. If not, give another on-leash time-out or tether the leash to a stable object and walk a foot or two away.

Simply ending playtime is an effective punishment for many puppies, since now your puppy has nothing and nobody to play with. You want him to think how boring it is when you stop playing with him (because he nipped you). This momentary social banishment is very effective. You are essentially telling your puppy that you will not play with him if he isn't careful with your skin.

After a week or so, the next step is to teach your pup to stop mouthing altogether. Some puppies will naturally decrease the frequency of their nips, especially when you have taught them to inhibit their force. When your puppy is 3 to 4 months old, it is time to teach him that he should not use his teeth on people at all. Using the same principle as when teaching bite inhibition, simply respond to any teeth on your skin (no matter how soft) with an end to the play session.

Don't Fight Fire with Fire

If your dog nips you, don't yell at him or go face to face to correct him. A hostile response might escalate the confrontation, or it might teach your puppy to hold back and wait to bite someone who isn't able to use force or scare him enough to stop (like a child). Certainly, don't grab for your dog's muzzle to correct him. This will only teach him not to like hands reaching toward his face.

Teaching Your Dog to Take Food Gently

Most dogs are naturally enthusiastic about food and may nip at your fingers when you offer them something. It is important to teach your dog to take food gently so that you and others may safely offer your dog food in response to good behavior and for the purpose of socialization. This is especially true for children. Your dog will make fast friends with children if they can offer him tasty treats from their hands.

If your dog takes food roughly, do not give him the food. Take your hand away and then bring it back to give your dog another chance to get the food. If he is more gentle the second time, open your hand and give him the treat. If not, take your hand away again. It may take many repetitions before your dog begins to understand how to get the food, but actions speak louder than words. So stay quiet and let your dog figure this out for himself. It may be helpful to have your dog on leash and tethered to a stable object so that you have both hands free and can stay just out of your dog's reach should you want to step away and give him a time-out from training.

You can also simply keep your hand still and closed around the bit of food that you offer to your dog. He will probably try to get the food out of your hand by mouthing it and pawing. By keeping your hand closed and still, you are telling your dog (without words) what doesn't work. He will eventually stop doing the behaviors that didn't work and pull back, at which point you should open your hand and give him the food. Repeat until he automatically backs off and waits for you to open your hand and offer him the treat. By doing so, he is showing you that he can control his impulses and be thoughtful and careful when accepting food.

Impulse Control

A great dog waits patiently and asks appropriately for what she wants. A demanding and impatient dog is likely to whine, bark, and jump to get what she wants. A dog in this state is similar to a child who is distraught over the injustice of not getting what she wants when she wants it—which is usually right now!

As a dog-friendly trainer, you recognize that while it is normal for a dog to want to access reinforcers (anything she wants) as directly and promptly as possible, a dog who behaves in this way is not likely to enjoy as many freedoms or be adored by all as she might be if she just learned a little self-control. Your dog needs to learn that the only way to get what she wants is to wait for you to give her permission. You are the source of all the things she wants, and the only way to get you (or anyone else) to give her those things is to remain calm and do as requested.

Developing your dog's self-control will facilitate a better relationship between you and potentially a longer and safer life for your dog, too. A dog with great self-control is much less likely to run through a doorway or out of a car door and onto the street where she may get hurt. She is also less likely to grab food from someone's hand and potentially cause injury by not being careful and thoughtful enough to take the food gently when given permission.

People who feel bad when they don't give a dog what she wants inadvertently encourage the dog's lack of self-control. This is a perfect example of killing with kindness—that is, trying to do right by a dog but ultimately teaching her very bad manners that will affect all aspects of her life.

Good Things Come to Those Who Wait

The main focus of teaching impulse control is to stop everything when your dog gets into a demanding frenzy. Ignore your dog completely, and be sure she gets no access to the thing she wants. If she gets herself into a tizzy at the front door demanding that you open it for her, for example, simply stop and wait. Remain perfectly still. It shouldn't take her long to figure out what she has to do to get you to open the door. When she remains still and quiet for a moment, mark with a click or by saying "yes" and reward her by opening the door. Likewise, as you prepare her meals, stop all preparations if she does anything other than wait calmly for you to finish. You can put the food out of your dog's reach and walk away. Walk back to the feeding area when your dog is calm with four feet on the floor. This may take many repetitions, but eventually your dog will learn to stay calm while food is being prepared.

Silence Is Golden

If your dog is being impulsive, it is best to ignore her completely and make sure that she has no access to what she desires. This way, she learns that those behaviors don't work. It may be difficult at first to teach this principle without saying words such as "off," "down," or "no," but the benefit of this silent way of teaching is that your dog will learn to stay calm without you having to say these things constantly.

Repetitions are the key to building physical muscles and learning muscles.

To follow are some excellent impulse-control exercises that you can begin to teach in a calm environment. As your dog masters these skills, practice them in more distracting areas and eventually implement them into your dog's daily routine. For example, teaching your dog not to touch a treat on the ground until given permission to do so can be an exercise that you repeat at mealtimes when you place your dog's food bowl or food-dispensing toy on the floor. Practicing these exercises in as many environments and as frequently as possible is the best way to develop a dog who understands that good things come to those who wait!

Since your dog is genetically predisposed to "take things now!" keep in mind that helping her learn to control her impulses in many different environments and scenarios will require many repetitions. For example, your dog might learn to show impulse control in the following exercises in your living room, but will need to essentially relearn how to control herself in more stimulating environments, such as on the street and around children and other dogs.

In addition to consistent repetition, be very generous with reinforcements so you convince your dog that waiting for something—which is typically not a natural instinct for dogs—is the best option.

Don't Encourage Impulsive Behavior!

Be careful not to accidentally decrease impulse control by:

✦ Giving your dog a meal after she jumps about as you prepare it.

✦ Allowing anyone to talk to your dog (even to say something like "off," which is negative, but is still attention) when she jumps up.

✦ Allowing anyone to talk to your dog when she barks.

✦ Allowing anyone to let your dog out of her crate, exercise pen, or any other enclosure when she is jumping, barking, or whining.

✦ Allowing anyone to give your dog a treat when she jumps for it or takes it in a rough manner. (You should not feel teeth on your hand.)

✦ Allowing your dog to greet or play with other dogs when she drags you toward them.

✦ Allowing your dog to grab things off counters and tabletops.

✦ Allowing your dog to grab things from your hand.

For Most Dogs, Negative Attention Is Better Than None at All

Talking to or even looking at your dog when she barks, whines, or jumps is likely to reinforce the behaviors happening at that moment. For most dogs, any attention—even negative attention, such as yelling "no"—can be very reinforcing, as it is better than no attention at all.

Time-outs are one of the most effective punishments. They tell your dog that whatever he was doing right before it happened resulted in him losing access to anything he wants, such as treats, toys, or your attention.

Impulse Control Exercises
Take the Jump out of That Bean

This exercise is an easy way to teach your dog to keep four feet on the ground when someone is holding food nearby. Hold a tiny treat about one foot above your dog's head. If your dog jumps for it, quickly lift your hand out of your dog's reach, and don't say a word. If your dog stays standing or sits for even one second, mark this behavior with a click or by saying "yes" and give her the treat.

Because you can repeat this game so quickly, you should be able to practice many repetitions in each three- to five-minute session. It usually takes just one or two sessions for your dog to understand that jumping makes the food go away and standing or sitting makes it appear. But your goal is to teach her to do so for as long as necessary—that is, not to jump for the food at all. When your dog is keeping four paws on the ground for a count of one, you can gradually increase the time you ask her to hold the position by delaying the mark and reward. Gradually increase the count to two, three, four, and so on, but be careful not to go too quickly, even if you have a super-smart dog. As with every training exercise, your goal is to set a solid foundation, which is best done slowly.

As you increase the duration you ask your dog to control herself, consider increasing the value of the reward. Maybe try using a tastier treat. Most important, be sure to be a generous rewarder. The pieces can be tiny, but should be offered frequently so that your dog learns how valuable it is to wait.

Actions Speak Louder Than Words

As a calm, gentle trainer, remind yourself that actions speak louder than words. Think of yourself as having an on/off switch that your dog can control with her behavior. Jumping, barking, and whining make you turn off, and sitting politely and waiting make you turn you on.

Wait, Please

There are two parts to teaching your dog to wait to touch food or other objects until given permission. If you practiced the anti–jumping bean exercise described above, you have already laid a foundation for this exercise.

1. Teach your dog not to touch things that you are holding.

2. Teach your dog not to touch things that you place on the ground or on another surface.

Start with number 1. Hold a piece of food in your closed hand. Ignore your dog when she pushes at your hand to get the food. Ignore everything she does to get at it (she may paw or bark). When she stops and backs off, click or say "yes," open your hand, and say "take it." To begin, even a momentary retreat should be marked and rewarded.

One of the foundations of impulse control is your dog learning not to charge for his food bowl until you have given him permission.

Gradually increase the length of time you ask your dog to avoid making contact with your hand before you mark and reward. When you feel confident that she understands what is expected, you can add a cue like "leave it." Say "leave it," present your closed hand, wait for your dog to back off, and then open your hand and say "take it." She'll learn that the only way to get the food after you say "leave it" is not to touch your hand.

To teach your dog not to touch a treat (or object) placed on the floor, sit on the floor next to your dog and ask her to sit or lie down. Place a piece of food on the ground about 12 inches away from your dog. If she gets up to take it (which she surely will), simply lift the food off the floor and either ignore your dog and wait for her to sit or lie down on her own, or ask her to. Place the food back on the ground and try again. If she refrains from going toward the food for even a moment (one second will do!), mark with a click or by saying "yes," and let her take the food. Gradually increase the length of time she is required to refrain from taking the food.

When you feel confident that your dog has a reliable understanding of and adherence to what is expected, you can start dropping the food on the ground from an inch or so above the floor. Gradually increase this distance until you are able to drop the treat from a standing position. If your pup forgets her manners and jumps up to get the food and you think you won't be quick enough to reach down to take it away, try stepping on it!

You can also work separately on decreasing the distance the food is away from your dog. But when doing so, be sure to decrease the time. For example, if your dog has a solid fifteen-second wait while the treat is

What terrific self-control!

12 inches away, start back at one or two seconds when you move the treat a few inches closer. Most dogs can master this challenge so well that you can eventually place the treat on their paw and they won't touch it until given permission to do so.

Yippee, You're Here!

When your dog is confined away from you in any manner (in her crate, tethered on a leash, behind a baby gate, or in another room), teach her that the only way to get you to approach is to keep all four feet on the floor. If she jumps, turn or walk away. When she has all four feet on the floor, start approaching again. As with all teaching, it will take many repetitions for your dog to figure out that keeping four feet on the floor is the way to get you to approach. You may find yourself walking back and forth for a few minutes until your dog is able to contain her enthusiasm.

On/Off Switch

In this game, you help your dog learn to show self-control in stimulating situations, such as around children or crowds. This on/off exercise is also a great opportunity to use play as a reward for self-control.

Start by playing with your dog in very short bursts separated by short periods of lying down. To begin, short sessions are best because some dogs will become overstimulated. As your dog masters the concept that lying down calmly is the way to get the game to start again, you can vary the length of time you play and ask your dog to lie down. Calming to a less aroused state is easier for some dogs than others, so it's important to have a good idea of what level your dog can handle and not to push her too far too fast. As with all dog-friendly training, your goal is to set your dog up to be successful.

Basic Manners

The five cornerstones of your dog's basic manners are sit, down, and stand (the position changes), plus hand targeting and the notion of closeness. By teaching these five things, you will be able to show your dog how to behave in nearly any circumstance. For example, you can ask him to sit to greet people politely, to lie down quietly while the family is eating, and to stand still while being examined by a veterinarian or groomer. Hand targeting enables you to redirect your dog's attention and gently and easily guide him where you want him to go. It is also a terrific exercise for ensuring that your dog is confident and enthusiastic about hands reaching toward him. Teaching your dog the desire to be close is the very essence of teaching him to walk calmly by your side down a busy street and to come back to you when you call him. Teaching these basics is vital to enjoying a fulfilling relationship with your dog, whether he is a tiny Chihuahua or an enormous St. Bernard.

The building blocks of basic manners are sit, down, stand, hand targeting, and come (the desire to be close).

When teaching basic manners, keep in mind the principles of dog-friendly dog training:

1. Always concentrate on teaching your dog what you want him to do. Remember, a reliable sit, down, stand, or hand target will prevent just about any behavior problem.

2. Until your dog is reliably trained, manage his lack of education; for example, keep him on leash and out of trouble.

3. Use gentle methods to teach your dog quickly and enjoyably. We all learn better when we are in a relaxed and happy state of mind.

Why Train Your Dog?

A well-trained dog gets much more out of life. You can take your dog just about anywhere with you and bask in the pride you feel when your well-trained dog is admired by one and all. All dogs, even the tiniest ones, must be taught to reliably respond to a few simple requests. The list of benefits to having a well-mannered dog is endless, including preventing a potential disaster if your dog gets off leash and does not come back when you call him.

Shirking the responsibility of training your new dog will only mean that you have to make a greater effort later on. Teaching your dog to respond to a few simple requests, such as sit, down, hand target, and come, is a great way to show him what you expect. This way, you can tell him what to do to be "right" in any given situation. For example, you can:

✦ Ask him to sit to greet people rather than jump on them.

✦ Ask him to lie down on his bed while your family eats dinner rather than get upset with him for begging at the table.

◆ Ask him to hand target rather than focus on another dog in the veterinarian's waiting room.

◆ Ask him to come to you when you call rather than get angry with him for running after the cat.

Did you get a dog so that your backyard could have a pet?

When you think about it, it would be really cruel *not* to train your dog. Training consists of showing your dog what you want him to do. It's too bad that many dogs are severely punished for behaviors their owners consider inappropriate, only because the owners didn't bother to show the dogs what was expected. The poor dogs end up being punished for breaking rules they didn't even know existed—all because of a lack of a little education and guidance.

English veterinarian and animal behaviorist Dr. Ian Dunbar considers training to be no different from teaching your dog ESL, or English as a Second Language. You're not teaching your dog to come, sit, and lie down. Eight-week-old puppies know how to come, sit, and lie down. Instead, you're teaching your dog the human signals (requests) for dog behaviors and actions. Wouldn't it be unfair to invite a social animal into your home only to relegate it to a communication void in solitary confinement? Of course, you must socialize and communicate with your dog. And rather than attempting to communicate by using a variety of dog languages, employing odors, body postures, and tail wags, training conveniently enables you to talk to your dog in your own language.

Training Happens All the Time

Training is not just time set aside for your dog's lessons. It's part of everyday life. In fact, your dog is learning every waking moment, whether or not you are there and whether or not you are intentionally training him.

Preparing to Teach

Good teachers prepare for class by creating a lesson plan and readying the classroom. This is the best way to optimize students' learning potential. A little preparation on your part will facilitate your dog's achievement of his full potential.

Choose the Classroom Carefully

Carefully choose the environment where you begin teaching your dog. Eventually, you'll want your dog to respond to your requests under all sorts of conditions, but when you begin teaching something new, it's best to train in an area with as few distractions as possible. This is usually in the quietest room in your home.

Precisely Define What You Want to Teach Your Dog

You should have a clear picture in your mind of what you are setting out to teach. Your lesson plan will be a precise definition of each word you intend to teach your dog. You don't have to use the same terms I use here (I have included some alternatives), but it is important to know precisely what you're trying to teach *before* you try to teach it.

A trained dog gets to be an integral part of the family.

For example, saying your dog's name might mean "pay attention," but how do you know for sure that he is paying attention? The best and most reliable way to assess this may be to see whether he looks at you. "Sit" might mean for your dog to immediately place his bottom on the ground exactly where he is and remain there until the next instruction is given, regardless of the situation and the level of distractions. "Down" might mean for your dog to immediately place his body on the ground exactly where he is and remain there until the next instruction is given, regardless of the situation and the level of distractions. "Walking nicely by your side" might mean that there should be no tension on the leash and the dog should remain on one side of you. "Come" might mean to run to you immediately when called and to either sit or remain close enough for you to grab his collar.

Think about how to apply the basic commands in everyday life so that you and your dog get the full benefit of this shared language.

Get Your Dog's Attention

It helps to be 0animated if you want to capture your dog's attention.

Before you can teach your dog anything, you must be sure that you can get your dog's attention. If you've followed the advice in Chapter 1 on controlling the resources in your dog's life, you'll find that your dog is already paying a whole lot of attention to you. Also, encourage your dog to make eye contact with you many times throughout the day, praising him for even momentary glances initially. Eventually, you should be able to get your dog's attention even in distracting circum-stances. But start to teach this in your home, without a lot of distractions.

What's in a Name?

One of the most important words to define for your dog is his name. When you say your dog's name, it should mean that you want him to pay attention and look at you since you are about to give further instructions.

Too many dogs think that their name means "bad dog." Be sure not to use your dog's name when you're unhappy with him. Moreover, if you repeat your dog's name over and over without consequence, he will even-tually learn to tune you out.

The best way to teach your dog to pay attention when you say his name is to hand-feed him his meals for a week. You don't have to hand-feed each and every piece of food, but the more pieces you hand-feed individually, the more dramatic the difference you will see in your dog's responsiveness to his name.

Say your dog's name in a happy, bright tone. The instant he looks at you, click or say "yes" and give him a piece of his meal. Within a few repetitions, your dog will start to understand that when he hears his name, he should look at you to hear the marker (click or "yes"), which means that he will get a reward.

Once your dog readily responds to his name by glancing at you, it is time to work toward increasing the duration of the glance. Your goal is to have a dog who is able to maintain attention (eye contact) for a reasonable period of time. Your dog should eventually be able to maintain eye contact for at least fifteen seconds.

Although a quick glance in your direction in response to his name was sufficient attention for a reward initially, now require your dog to look at you for two seconds before clicking or saying "yes" to mark the behavior of looking at you and focusing his attention on you for two seconds and then rewarding him. Next time, you might wait for him to look at you for three seconds. In upcoming three- to five-minute training sessions, you can gradually increase to five seconds, eight seconds, ten seconds, and so on. Before you know it, your dog won't take his eyes off you.

Now move to different rooms in the house. When you move into areas with more distractions, you'll need to increase the rewards until he gives you attention there. Your goal is to teach your dog to look at you when he sees a distraction, as it is an opportunity for more reinforcement.

Eventually, when your dog reliably understands to look at you and focus until you ask him to do something else, repeat the process without food or other rewards on your person. Instead, say his name, and when he looks at you, let him know what a great dog he is. Occasionally, go get a reward (food, a toy, or his leash to take him for a walk!).

Remedial Action

What if your dog doesn't look at you when you say his name? Ignore him and play with a toy he likes a lot. If he tries to join in, continue to ignore him. Or produce something yummy and eat it yourself. Then try again!

Training Game for Attention

Ask a friend or family member to be your assistant in this game. Give her some food to hold while you have something your dog loves in your pocket. Sit a few feet apart. Have your assistant show your dog the food distraction, but she must not give it to the dog. When the dog is distracted by the food, say your dog's name. If your dog looks at you, mark the behavior with a click or "yes" and offer the high-level reward you were hiding, plus the food distraction from your assistant as an additional reward (you can use very tiny pieces).

If your dog does not look at you, walk over to him and show him what you had to offer him. Let him know how bad you feel for him that he missed out on getting it. Sit down and completely ignore your dog for a minute. Then have your assistant distract him again, and you say his

Teach your dog that coming when called is a fun game by calling him back and forth between family members who praise and reward him for each correct response.

name again. Chances are that you will get his full attention this time. By having your assistant never actually give your dog any food, she is helping you to show him that paying attention to this distraction is no good. You are the only slot machine that is rewarding in this casino!

Choose a Release Word

Unless you expect your dog to look at you or stay in a position forever, you'll need to choose a word that means he is released and is essentially on his own time. A lot of people use "okay" or "all done." From here on, you will be teaching your dog that the only time he is released is when you have given another command, given his release word, or marked a behavior with the clicker or the word "yes," which means that he has accomplished the behavior you wanted and is done. The clearer you are in this regard, the easier you will make things for your dog. It will confuse him if you sometimes allow him to get up from a sit before you have said the release word and then other times get frustrated and reprimand him for doing so.

A great way to teach your dog that training is fun is to ignore him when you release him. You want your dog to beg you to ask him to do something else so that he has another opportunity to interact with you and be rewarded. You want a dog who loves to be in the training game, not a dog who anticipates being released.

So, when you begin teaching any of the basic positions (sit, down, and stand), be sure to say "okay," "all done," or whichever release words you choose to let your dog know that he may move. At first, this will be after a one-second position hold, but you will gradually build up to three, five, ten seconds and more before you release.

Teach your dog his release cue simply by saying it and then calmly encouraging him to move. If you are using a clicker and/or the word "yes," note that this marker lets your dog know that he is all done as well. You can offer the food reward from your hand or drop it on the ground to encourage your dog to move out of the position he was in.

Reasons to Teach Sit, Down, and Stand

Sit

Most people can think of at least a few reasons for teaching a dog to sit. For example, you want your dog to sit instead of jump on people or to sit rather than run out the door. There are, however, many other uses for this position. In fact, a reliable sit is probably the most underrated and underused command in the dog world. Aside from socialization, "sit" is the best way to prevent and solve many behavior problems, including lunging when on leash, chewing inappropriate items, harassing the cat, barking, and overall lack of impulse control (see Chapter 6).

Good Times to Sit

- At the front door (going in and out)
- When greeting people
- While meals are being prepared
- In elevators
- Every 20 to 30 feet on a walk
- Before being let off leash
- Frequently during play sessions and games
- Before you throw a tennis ball or disc
- Before all good times (such as couch privileges)

Down

Generally, you use "down" to instruct your dog to remain in position for longer periods, such as in the living room while guests are getting settled and a lot of activity is happening. "Down" is also an aid for housetraining. By asking your dog to settle down for a lengthy period, you can accurately predict when he needs to go to his doggy toilet (when he gets up) and take him there to reward him when he goes. "Down" may also be used as an emergency command (for example, if your dog gets off leash, you can ask him to lie down to get him under control and back on leash) and to prevent a slew of unwanted and annoying behaviors.

Good Times to Down

✦ Whenever a sit would be inappropriate (such as
 when you need the dog to be stationary for a long period)

✦ Every 20 to 30 feet on walks to ensure that he is attentive to you

✦ To calm an overexcited dog

✦ In the waiting room at the veterinarian's office

✦ During your meals

Stand

"Stand" is the easiest position for examining and grooming your dog. If your
dog stands still, your veterinarian and groomer will absolutely love you.

It's also vital to teach a third position change. Stand is a wonderful
choice. If you teach just sit and down and alternate between them (sit,
down, sit, down, as in doing puppy push-ups), the dog learns to anticipate
the next position. If he is sitting, the next position will be down. In this
case, your dog doesn't actually learn the meaning of the words, but rather
that one behavior leads to the next predictable behavior. So each time
you ask your dog to sit, he is likely to predict that down is next and go
right into it. But if you teach at least three positions, your dog has to wait
for the appropriate instruction. With three body positions to choose from,
from each position there are two that you might ask for. For example,
from a sit, you can ask your dog for a down or a stand, from a down you
can ask for a sit or a stand, and from a stand you can ask for a sit or a
down. So, by teaching three position changes, you are actually training
the dog to pay attention and really learn what the words mean.

Good Times to Stand

✦ While being examined at the veterinarian's office

✦ While being bathed and groomed

✦ When being petted by a person in a chair on a therapy visit to a hospital or nursing home

---

Preparation Checklist: Teaching the Basics

✓ Carefully choose the classroom.

✓ Precisely define the words you teach your dog.

✓ Teach your dog to pay attention when you say his name.

✓ Teach your dog a release word.

If you've accomplished all four of these steps, then you and your dog are ready to move on.

The Six Position Changes

Remember that when you are teaching three body positions, you're actually teaching six position changes:

1. Stand to sit
2. Stand to down
3. Sit to down
4. Sit to stand
5. Down to sit
6. Down to stand

Some changes are easier or more difficult than others. For example, it's easy to get a dog to stand or lie down when sitting; it's much harder to get him to sit when lying down or to lie down from the standing position. Luckily, lure/reward training (see page 163) makes the process easier, and there is no better way to teach rapid position changes.

The Six Position Changes

Stand to Sit

Sit to Down

Down to Stand

Stand to Down

Down to Sit

Sit to Stand

Name It When Your Dog Knows It!

Reward-based trainers differ from traditional trainers in that they wait until the animal understands a behavior well before using a verbal command, or *cue*. A cue is the name you give a behavior, such as "sit." Until your dog knows the behavior, it is useless to try to teach him a word for the behavior. You'll just end up saying "sit, sit, sit!" with no response since your dog doesn't know what you want.

When your dog confidently repeats a behavior in response to a hand lure or offers the behavior automatically, and you are sure that he understands what he has to do to get a reward, he is ready to learn the cue for the behavior. Teach your dog the cue by saying or doing it right before he repeats the behavior. For example, if your dog is sitting promptly and reliably after you take a step and stop, you know that the next time you do so he is likely to sit. So say "sit" right before you stop. As always, repetition and reinforcement are the keys to your dog understanding to listen for the cue that tells him to sit.

The Three Methods for Teaching Sit, Down, and Stand

There are three methods for teaching your dog the basics:

+ Capturing/shaping

+ Lure/reward training

+ Physical prompting

Capturing

Capturing is an exceptionally good method of training. One neat thing about it is that you are creating a dog who is a great problem solver—a terrific quality in any student. You're letting your dog know, "I've got

something you want here; what do you think you have to do to get it?"
Then you just wait until the dog works it out himself and gets it right. It's
a fun little game, and dogs love it.

Basically, this is the method of choice for just about all dogs, including
rambunctious dogs, fearful dogs, and aggressive dogs (in other
words, dogs who don't yet like being touched). Although
time-consuming at first, once you get going and your dog
understands that he has to figure out what is expected in order
to get the reward, training will move along like gang-
busters. This is a great way to teach your dog to do just
about anything, from sitting on cue to com-
pleting a complicated series of tricks. In
fact, animals you see in the movies and
commercials are all trained in this way.
Capturing and shaping creates a dog who per-
forms reliably and happily.

To begin, you simply stay quiet and wait for your dog to offer a
behavior you want. The moment it happens, you mark with a click
of your clicker or by saying "yes" and reward.

The wonderful thing about capturing and shaping is that you just amuse yourself and wait for your dog to figure out what you want.

Sit

To teach your dog to sit, hold a handful of your dog's dry food or special
treats and wait for him to sit. Don't say a word; let him figure out what he
has to do to get what you have. You can speed things up if you keep your
dog on a leash. Step on it so it's just long enough for your dog to stand,
sit, and lie down comfortably. If you just stand still, your dog is likely to

throw his entire behavioral repertoire at you—he may paw, bark, and so on. Ignore behaviors other than sitting. The first sit may take a few minutes, but don't lose your patience during this initially slow part of an otherwise rapid process. Pretty soon he'll sit. Mark the moment his rear hits the ground with the clicker or by saying "yes" and give him the reward.

How Many Miles per Gallon, How Many Sits per Piece of Food?

Get the most out of your dog's food. Most owners go to the kitchen and prepare their dog's dinner while he goes crazy bouncing all over. Then the owner rewards this behavior by giving the dog dinner. Instead, ask your dog for a few sit, stand, and down repetitions before you give him his dinner. Better yet, spend five minutes using a few individual pieces of food to get your dog to play the training game with you. See how many sits or downs you can get for each piece.

The click means the end of the behavior, so your dog may have gotten up already, but you can say your release word to remind him that he is free to move about, take one step away from him, and wait for him to sit again. The sit should occur in a little less time than the last. By the time you have done six to ten sits, the dog will be sitting instantaneously each time you stop. He will have figured out which "button to push" to get you to release a piece of food.

Once you can predict when your dog will sit (when you stop), you are ready to say "sit" right before you think it will happen (when you stop). This way, you are beginning to teach your dog the verbal cue for sitting.

Down and Stand

The technique for the sit also applies to down and stand. Work on each of these behaviors separately. Simply wait for your dog to "give" you these behaviors, and promptly reward him for doing so. As with teaching "sit," it may take a few moments for your dog to offer the first down or stand. But after you mark and reward the first offering of either behavior, each one is likely to be offered more quickly thereafter. After six to ten repetitions, your dog is likely to have figured out that lying down and standing in front of you are "buttons to push" to get you to release a piece of food.

Once you can predict when your dog will lie down or stand (when you stop), you are ready to say "down" or "stand" right before you think either behavior will happen.

Lure/Reward Training

Sit

Basically, by luring your dog to move his nose, the rest of his body will follow. So, if you hold a piece of food in your hand and slowly lift it upward and backward over your dog's nose, passing it between his eyes, his rear end will descend into the sitting position as he looks up to follow the food. Mark with a click or "yes" and give him a tiny treat. When you are confident that he will follow your hand movement into the sit position, you can predict when the sit will happen. So say "sit" before you move the lure, and click or say "yes" the moment his rear touches the ground and then give the reward. Again, the marker says that the behavior is done and he is free to move, but you can also say your release word as a reminder. Be careful not to add the cue word (in this case, "sit") until you are confident that the desired behavior will happen when you move your hand up and back. Otherwise, you are simply saying a word ("sit"), and it is not being connected with a behavior.

So that your dog learns to do a reliable sit on request regardless of his body position in relation to yours (that is, not just in front of you), practice this exercise with him in as many variations as possible, including him at your side, you in a chair, and him lying down.

Practice, Practice, Practice

Once you've taught your dog the position changes, you can practice many, many times throughout the day. Three- to five-minute training sessions are best. Just ask your dog to come and do a few position changes for a few tiny, tasty treats, or for the privilege of getting on the couch, or before you throw a tennis ball.

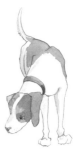

Down

To get your dog to lie down, hold your hand with the food lure in it in front of his nose and move it straight down to the ground and slightly in toward his chest. Your dog will fold down like a table as his nose follows the lure, and so will his forequarters. Usually, a dog will lie down completely at this point. If he does, mark the moment his stomach is flat on the ground with a click or by saying "yes" and give him the tiny piece of food. If the dog's nose and forequarters go down but his rear end is still sticking up in the air, however, push the food lure gently toward his chest a little more, and as your dog pushes back to sniff, his rear end will collapse to the ground.

Getting your dog to lie down may take a few tries. Try working on a slippery surface to begin. This will make it much easier to get your dog to slide to the ground. But don't let him have the lure until he is lying down. He can sniff at your hand, but keep it closed around the food lure. Don't say anything. He will eventually lie down, and then you can click or say "yes" and open your hand to give him the food. Release him and repeat the routine many times in each three- to five-minute training session.

There is a trick for luring little or short-legged dogs into a down. Simply place your dog at the top of a flight of stairs and position yourself one step down. Use your hand with the lure to guide the dog's head below the stair. After a few repetitions on the stairs, you and your pooch will be ready to try it on a flat surface. You can also entice your dog to lie down by luring him to crawl under your bent leg.

Stand

To teach your dog to stand on command, move the food from in front of the dog's nose to where his nose would be if he were standing. If your dog does not stand up, waggle the treat a little, and soon he will rise. When he stands, immediately mark with a click or a "yes" and give the reinforcement.

Five Steps to Eliminating the Lure

While lures can be useful in training, your goal should be to use 'em and lose 'em as fast as possible. To phase out food (or other lures), simply stop holding the lure in your hand. You will find that if you make the same hand movement you did when you held a food lure, you have a hand signal! So the dog learns hand signals very quickly. Mark the behavior and offer a treat from the other hand as a reward. If he doesn't respond to the empty-handed hand signal, simply try again.

The five steps to eliminating the use of a lure in training are:

1. Lure in hand, reward every time.

2. No lure in hand, reward from other hand every time.

3. No lure in hand, reward from other hand randomly.

4. No lure in hand, someone else hands you the reward or you get the reward from someplace else.

5. No lure in hand; use life rewards most of the time, like continuing a walk, verbal praise, and petting; offer the occasional food reward.

Rover Rollover

Teaching your dog to roll over as a trick is a gentle way to get him to tolerate and even enjoy being in a vulnerable position, which he might not otherwise be comfortable with. The lure/reward method is a good choice for teaching a dog to roll over. Lure your dog into a down, and then use the lure to guide his head to the ground so that he's lying flat on one side. Now move the lure over your dog's shoulder so that he must twist his neck a bit to follow it. When his feet start to go up, move the lure a little more quickly. When he rolls all the way over, mark with a click or "yes" and open your hand to give him a small piece of the lure as a reward while he's still lying down. Once your dog has begun to roll over quickly when you use your hand to lure him, add the words "roll over" as you lure your dog. Remember that this is a vulnerable position for your dog, so don't lose patience if it takes a little while for him to feel confident enough to roll over. Some dogs are more comfortable learning this trick first on a soft surface (such as a rug or a towel) and then working on regular flooring.

Physical Prompting

Many people are familiar with the techniques to physically prompt a dog to sit, lie down, and stand. If done correctly, the dog may learn when touched on the rump or when gently touched between his shoulders to assume the appropriate position. At first, the methods seem to get a quick response, but, in fact, physical prompting is surprisingly time-consuming and not nearly as effective or fun as the other two approaches. Because touch is so important to dogs, your dog will selectively attend to the touch. In effect, he doesn't even hear the instructions you give. Teaching your dog verbal commands from the outset using capturing and shaping or lure/reward training is much more effective.

One of the drawbacks of physical prompting is that dogs learn they can do what they like when they are out of reach.

Maintain a Good Attitude

Your dog's enthusiasm for learning depends greatly on you, so never try to train if you're feeling irritable.

Teaching Your Dog to Stay

Using a word to tell your dog to stay is repetitive if you have already decided to teach your dog that the words "sit," "down," and "stand" mean to stay in position until released or asked to do something else. But feel free to use the word "stay" if it makes you happy.

A sit-stay is useful when something is going on and you need short-term control. A down-stay is useful for long-term control. A stand-stay is helpful for having your dog stand still for an examination or grooming.

Using the capturing and lure/reward methods, just wait to reward for the sits, downs, or stands that are incrementally longer. Pure simplicity!

For example, ask your dog to sit, and mark and reward him when he does. The next time, wait for your dog to remain sitting for a full second before marking and rewarding. If your dog gets up beforehand, just ask him to sit and try again. It should not take him long to figure out (without you yelling "stay!") that staying in position is the way to get the reward.

When your dog is staying reliably for one second, wait for two seconds of sitting before marking and rewarding. Then go for three seconds, five, eight, ten, fifteen, twenty, and so on. Vary the length of time you ask your dog to stay, sometimes decreasing to a level far below your goal.

For example, if he is becoming

Hands-off reward methods create a good foundation for off-leash distance control.

reliable with a thirty-second down-stay, you should still frequently ask and reward him for three- to ten-second stays. With this approach, it will surprise you how quickly your dog learns quite lengthy stays.

As you make any task more difficult, be sure to follow it with an extra-generous reward. So, if your dog is holding a stay for fifteen seconds for the first time, he might deserve a jackpot reward of three tiny treats as opposed to the typical one.

Proofing Stays

The process of *proofing* your dog's stays—or making sure that he focuses on you no matter what the circumstances—comprises the three D's:

◆ Increasing the **duration**

◆ Increasing the **distractions**

◆ Increasing the **distance** between you and your dog

Eventually, your dog will understand that he is to stay in position for an extended period when there are numerous distractions, while he remains a distance away from you. But you need to work on each component separately and gradually. Building duration, distractions, and distance is like turning up the volume on a stereo. If you raise the level too high too fast, your dog won't be able to concentrate on what you are asking him to do. Make things easier on yourself and your dog: go slowly.

When you increase the difficulty of one D, decrease the difficulty of another. So if you have built up to a reliable ten-second stay and are now working on adding a distraction, be sure to decrease the duration to a brief moment or two. Basically, with each increase in duration, added distraction, or added bit of distance, you are asking more of your dog. So do your best to set him up for success by making some other part of the equation easier, whether it be lessening the other D's or increasing the value of the rewards your dog can earn.

Doubles, Anyone?

Playing the training game with two handlers at once can be very helpful, especially if you are working on distance and distractions. One person can stay next to the dog to help and reward him, while the other person moves a distance away and/or creates distractions.

Increasing the Duration

By simply delaying the reward, you will increase the length of time your dog stays in the required position. Hold on to that piece of food for two seconds and mark the behavior of staying in that position with a click or a "yes" and reward. Then see if you can hold on to the kibble for four seconds. If your dog gets up, either ask him to get back into position (sit, down, or stand) again or simply ignore him and wait for him to figure it out. (This is another time when it's good to have your dog on a leash that you're stepping on or that's connected to a stationary object.)

Increasing the Distractions

Start training your dog with as few distractions as possible. Then gradually increase them, one by one, until your dog responds reliably no matter what the distraction.

Start with a very mild distraction. What is considered mild will vary from dog to dog. For some, the presence of a tennis ball rolling across the floor is enough to send them sky-rocketing to the moon, while others wouldn't bat an eye. You know your dog best, so start off with something he isn't very interested in.

As you add distractions, increase the rewards and decrease the length of time. For example, for a dog who is able to do a nice thirty-second sit without new distractions, ask for a three-second sit in the presence of a tennis ball. At the same time, lavishly praise him and offer a nice food reward for his success.

Remember, stays are much harder for your dog in the presence of a single distraction. So keep the distance and duration short and up the level of rewards.

Increasing the Distance

When you work on building up the distance you can walk away from your dog while he is sitting or lying down, remove distractions and decrease the length of time you ask him to hold a position. Move just one step away, and mark with a click or by saying "yes" and reward with a tiny treat if he stays. If he gets up, step back and ask him to sit or lie down again or wait for him to do so. Take a tiny step away again, and go right

When proofing stays, increase your distance from your dog gradually and progressively.

back to praise and reward him if he stays put. The next time, step two steps away for a short period. Then try three steps, five, eight, ten, and so on until you can walk far away and your dog stays put.

Gradually increase the distance you move away, and don't forget to increase the rewards as you ask for more difficult behavior. If at any point your dog gets up, don't get mad at him. Calmly ask him for the appropriate position once more, or wait for him to figure out that he needs to offer it on his own.

Time and Training

Keep training sessions short, and stop while your dog still wants to play the training game. Short and frequent sessions are the best policy. Twenty-five three-minute training sessions a day will give you and your dog ample opportunity to build up reliability, even around enticing distractions. Setting aside an hour-long training session for your dog each day isn't very realistic or effective. Doing so can make the process seem long and boring for you and your dog. Having a specific training time is great, but remember that your dog is really being trained every waking moment, whether you're there or not.

Just to Be Close to You

Instilling in your dog the desire to be close to you is at the heart of teaching him to come when you call and walk nicely by your side on leash. Because proximity is a sign of affection and confidence, you will have a much easier time teaching your dog to come close (recall) and stay close (walk nicely on leash) if he trusts, likes, and wants to be near you. If your dog ignores you or runs away when you call him, it tells you where you are in the relationship. In this case, you simply need to give yourself and your dog a fresh start. If you have lived together for a while, pretend as though you just brought him home and follow the instructions beginning on the next page. Using dog-friendly training techniques all but assures that you and your dog will develop a loving and trusting bond and that your dog will want to be close. A dog who likes to be close to you and has been adequately rewarded for doing so will respond enthusiastically when you call him to come or to walk by your side.

It's very easy to instill in young puppies a desire to be close that will carry through to adulthood. Young puppies (especially those under 4 months old) have a strong tendency to follow anything that moves away. It is wise to imprint off-leash control before this time. If your pup doesn't choose to be close to you by 4½ months, then you'd better get on the ball.

On/Off Switch

Stop play sessions often to ask your dog to sit or lie down before starting play again. You'll ensure that you can get your dog's attention even at the height of excitement. Moreover, excited play becomes a reward for responding to your request rather than a distraction.

Come When Called

Teaching your dog to come when called is one of the most important obedience exercises you'll ever teach. It's the best way to allow your dog to safely enjoy off-leash fun, but more important, a good recall is the best way to prevent potential disasters. The consequences of a dog who ignores you when off leash can be devastating. Your goal with this exercise is to teach your dog to come to you even in the face of very enticing distractions. You are teaching him that it is always better to go to you than to anything or anyone else.

Choose and Use Your Recall Word Wisely

The word you use to ask your dog to come to you should be special and should be given top priority. So choose and use it carefully. If you have a dog with whom you have already used the word "come" and he ignores it, then you may want to choose a new word and start fresh.

Sit at the End

At the end of a recall, it is a good idea to add a sit. Why? Because a motivated, fast-paced recall from a medium or large dog may mean that he runs right into you or past you. So make sure that your dog knows to end up in a sit. Show your dog that you have a great treat or toy as he is about three dog lengths away from you so that he can slow down in anticipation of sitting to get it.

Someday, your dog's life may depend on his knowing to come to you when called, so don't ruin his recall word by using it before you have taught your dog to want to run to you. Start by saying this word only when you're as sure as possible that your dog will respond. Do not begin by using it when your dog is off leash in an area where you are less interesting than the environment, or another dog's rear end! If he chooses not to respond, then you have allowed your dog at least one opportunity to learn that he doesn't have to respond. Instead, keep your dog on leash or in a safely enclosed area until you have taught him to come when called. Also, don't call your dog if you are about to do something he finds unpleasant, such as bathe him, clip his nails, or take him home from a run in the park. Instead, calmly walk over, get a hold of his collar, and give him a treat (which should be easy if you've practiced handling your dog and worked on the "Gotcha!" exercise). This way, you avoid associating the recall with unpleasant things and thereby increase the chance that your dog will respond to you when you do call him (especially in an emergency) in the future.

Guaranteed Recall

Call your dog at least five times a day for a week when you're sure he will come. This usually means in the house at a close distance, or when he is already coming toward you. Reward him with the best things to happen to him that day (play, hugs, treats, a walk).

Play Hide-and-Seek

No matter which techniques you use to teach your dog to come when called, you should make things easier on yourself and your dog by instilling in your dog the desire to keep his eye on you and want to come close. Playing hide-and-seek with your dog is a great way to do this.

There are two variations of hide-and-seek, and both are great for the whole family to play. The first variation has the greatest impact on puppies under 4½ months old, because they are so impressionable. It is best to play this game in a safely enclosed area, preferably in your house or yard. The next best option is a friend's house or yard or a dog-training school.

Let your puppy get distracted, and when he does, run and hide. Wait until he notices that you are gone and starts looking for you. Give him a few moments to try to find you. If you see that he is really concerned, make a little noise to give him an idea of where you are. After a few moments, jump out and let your puppy know where you are. Hug him and praise him when he finds you. This exercise is almost one-trial learning. Your dog will learn that sticking close to you is important, because you have a tendency to get lost!

The second variation can be played indoors or outdoors in a safely enclosed area. When your dog is distracted, call his name and then

Here Henry!

Hiding from your dog in safe places is one of the best exercises to teach him to pay attention and stay close.

run a little ways away so that he is enticed to run to you for hugs and kisses. If you can't "lose" your dog, put something on the floor (a bit of food) to distract him and then run and hide. To begin, go only a short distance away. As he gets the knack of the game, you can move farther away and practice in more distracting areas.

Ready, Set, Go!

Have a friend or family member hold onto your dog as you dash off. Call your dog to you when you get about 20 feet away. When your dog is coming to you reliably, start to add distractions. Try setting out a couple of toys that your dog must pass on his way to get to you. When he does get to you, reward him by having even better toys for him to play with and a few tiny, tasty treats.

Use Capturing/Shaping to Teach Your Dog to Come

This method could be called No-Call Recalls! As with all capturing training, this process is so easy that you may not believe it works until you see it for yourself. All you need to do is wait for your dog to approach you and mark and reward him when he does. There is no need to call him to you yet. He will learn that the simple act of heading in your direction is likely to produce a very happy person and maybe even a tasty piece of food. Be sure to be very generous with rewards since this behavior is very important for your dog to learn. Also, vary what you offer as a reward, as this is the best way to keep your dog interested in the training game.

After a week or so of practicing, call your dog once you see that he's heading toward you (this is where the verbal instruction comes in). After another few days, try calling him right before he chooses to run to you on his own.

Use Lure/Reward Training to Teach Your Dog to Come

Stand or sit in a chair across from a family member or friend. Call your dog to you and encourage him to come toward you by showing him a lure (a toy or treat). Praise him starting with the very first step he takes in your direction. When he gets to you, give him a tiny piece of the treat. Then have the person in the chair opposite you call him the same way. Be sure to ignore your dog once the other person calls him.

To keep the game interesting, have a few different rewards to offer, and don't repeat this exercise more than six to ten times in a given play session. Move farther and farther apart and continue to reward. As your

Ping-Pong recalls are a wonderful way to attract your dog's attention.

dog gets better at the game, reward randomly and keep him guessing about what the reward will be.

Another lure/reward technique is to find a friend with a well-trained dog. Call your dog and then have your friend, who should be standing next to you, call her dog immediately after. Her dog will come running, and your dog will follow! Pretty soon your dog will get the idea, and you can speed both dogs up by rewarding the first one to get to you with a treat. By doing so, you will get some very fast-moving dogs. If one dog simply can't move as quickly as the other, you can level the playing field by waiting until the slower dog is closer to you when you call them.

The very best way to speed up recalls: two dogs but only one treat!

Don't Use Physical Prompting to Try to Teach Your Dog to Come

A lot of people will teach a dog to come on a long line, and of course using a leash helps to ensure your dog's safety. So you should have a leash on your dog anytime it is likely to keep him safe and set him up to be successful. However, I strongly recommend using the leash only for safety, and not to rely on the leash to teach your dog to come. If you do so, you

When your dog is on a long line, it is possible to safely teach recalls in public places.

COME !

are setting yourself up for failure. Everything goes fine when you are doing recalls on leash—when you can drag the dog to you like a dead sea bass, you know that he's going to come. This becomes a tremendous crutch in training, and neither you nor the dog is developing off-leash skills.

Shake, Rattle, and Call

Always have a few bits of food in your pocket when your puppy or adult dog is in training. If you don't like carrying food around, you can keep it in screw-top jars in strategic places like on the fridge, in the bathroom, or in the garden near his doggy toilet. Whenever you pass one of these jars, you can call the dog and then shake the jar. When he comes, get out a piece of kibble and give it to him. After a while, you'll want to thin out the number of times you shake the jar after you call him and the number of times you give him a piece of food. This way, you will have a dog who comes when you call him, even if you don't have a treat on you.

How to Guarantee That Your Dog Won't Come

The recall is one of the easiest commands to teach but one of the quickest to trash. Many owners ruin their dog's desire to come when called by doing one or all of the following:

+ Calling an off-leash dog to come before he is trained

+ Calling the dog when they're about to do something he doesn't like (for example, nail clipping or bathing)

+ Calling the dog when they're angry

+ Calling the dog to be put in confinement

+ Waiting to praise the dog until he gets to them

+ Not rewarding the dog sufficiently

+ Calling the dog to put on his leash at the dog park

Obviously, don't do any of these things!

When a dog doesn't come when called, first catch the dog. For his own safety, please don't let him off leash again until you have trained him to be more reliable.

Your dog isn't going to come quickly the next time if you yell at him when he gets there. Always reward your dog when he gets to you.

Encourage your dog to check in with you frequently anytime he is allowed to be off leash in a safely enclosed area. You can clap your hands or make a kissy noise to get his attention. When he heads toward you, let him know how pleased you are and then tell him to go back and play again. You are accomplishing two important things here: checking to make sure that your dog complies and teaching your dog that coming to you does not mean the end of play, but rather a pleasant time-out for a reward.

Maintaining a Great Recall

Don't wait until an emergency to call your dog; you may find that he isn't trained as well as you thought. Keeping your dog's recall reliable is a top priority. Call your dog to you no less than ten times a day, every day, and vary the rewards from verbal praise to a tasty treat or a game of fetch. Remember to praise your dog every step of the way as he heads in your direction. Neglecting to praise your dog while he is in the act of coming to you is a surefire way to teach him not to run to you.

Walk Nicely on Leash

Pulling on the leash seems to be a very enjoyable activity for most dogs. After all, so many dogs do it! And while you certainly want your dog to

Be aware! The biggest distraction for all sight hounds (in fact, for most dogs) is a rapidly retreating critter. If you don't yet have a reliable recall, walk your dog on leash.

have fun when taken out for a walk, you want to have a good time, too! Even a small to medium-sized dog who pulls is unpleasant and potentially dangerous, especially in the hands of a child or senior citizen. As a result, many owners walk their pulling dogs less. And when the dog is rarely walked, he is more excited than ever when he finally is walked. But once you teach your dog to walk nicely by your side, you will want to take him on lots of walks, even to places crowded with people.

Your goal is to teach your dog that whenever he's on leash and the leash is attached to you, he should pay attention and follow you. A tight leash acts as a telegraph wire for your dog to know where you are without having to watch you, so a slack leash is what you are aiming for.

Lots of people ask me if it's okay to let their dogs pull sometimes. Many people seem to think that not allowing their dog to pull is a tragedy for the dog. If you teach your dog to walk nicely without pulling on the leash, he will be happier because you will probably want to walk him more! But if you want your dog to pull you sometimes (up steep hills, for example), you can teach him to pull on command. But first focus on developing in your dog a strong habit of walking with a slack leash.

Three Points Before You Begin Leash Training

1. Have at least three great rewards (toys and treats) ready to use to teach your dog to walk by your side.

2. Be sure that you have done some groundwork on attention. To get your dog to follow you, you must first be able to get his attention.

3. Remember that it takes two to have a leash tug-of-war. Your job is to make sure that the leash is always loose. When you do your best to keep the leash loose, your dog has to pay attention to see where you are going. If you don't have the time or inclination to do your part to avoid a pulling game at that moment, then use a head halter to help inhibit pulling. Don't undo all your work when you can't pay attention to your dog. Remember, if there is tension on the leash, there isn't much attention from your dog or from you.

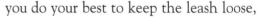

Even dogs who have been bred to pull can be taught to walk nicely on leash.

Teach Your Dog to Follow the Leader

Regardless of which training method you use, teaching your dog to walk nicely *on* leash is much easier to do if you have first taught him to want to stay close to you when he is *off* leash. After all, if your dog stays by your side without you having to keep him there with a leash, then you know he *wants* to be there. So the first step is to play the following game. Inside your home and in safely enclosed outdoor areas, walk around and encourage your dog to follow you by rewarding him when he does with toys, praise, special treats, and his normal food.

The rules of the game are simple: Walk away from your dog and reward him when he follows. The moment you see him move in the direction you move, mark with a click or "yes" and offer a tiny treat. By walking away from your dog, you will essentially be attempting to use yourself as an enticing lure. You can also stop occasionally to encourage him to play with you or with a toy. If he doesn't follow, do anything you can think of to get his attention. Speed up, squeak a squeaky toy, or make a clapping noise. This dog is telling you that he doesn't find you very interesting, so liven up! You'll both have more fun!

Use Capturing/Shaping in Leash Training

You don't even need to say a word to teach your dog to walk nicely by your side. If you look back at the technique to teach your dog to sit, you'll see that you can use capturing and shaping techniques to teach him to . . .

+ Sit quickly
+ Remain in the sit-stay
+ Walk by your side without pulling on leash when you walk

. . . all in one exercise!

When using motivation-based training, even children can master dog-friendly dog training!

When your dog pulls on the leash and bounces all over, stop and wait for him to settle and sit. Don't say a word. This usually takes a minute or so. He may go through a whole repertoire (pulling, barking, and circling) to get you to move. Ignore his antics and wait for the sit. Tell him "thank you" when he does sit, mark with the clicker or by saying "yes," and give him a piece of food. Then take one step. Wait until he sits again, give him another piece of food, and then take another step.

It should take progressively less time for him to sit each time. You'll notice how energized he gets with just one step, so don't try to speed things up too much and take more than one step until he has done at least ten one-step sits, sitting immediately each time.

Your dog will quickly learn that watching you and staying by your side is the only way to make the walk continue and get a treat. The more he wants something (in this case, the walk or the treat), the harder he will try to figure out how to get it (in this case, by sitting).

Now that you have piqued your dog's interest, you can move on to taking a couple of steps, and then stop and wait for another sit. Within a few days, you should be able to take your dog for a walk and stop only every 10 feet or so for a sit to reward your dog for walking nicely on leash.

If your dog pulls on leash, don't continue to move forward, as each step you take rewards your dog for pulling. Instead, stop, wait for your dog to come back to your side, and then continue to walk so your dog learns that sticking close by is the way to get the walk to continue.

Use the Lure/Reward Technique in Leash Training

Using the lure/reward technique to teach your dog to walk by your side is simple. Hold some treats in your hand and wiggle them in front of your dog to let him sniff them. Your dog will walk by your side sniffing at the treats. Take one step forward, stop, ask your dog to sit, and, with your right hand, give him a sit signal (raise your hand up a little and toward the back of his head so he looks up and his rear end goes down). Give him the treat when he sits, wiggle your left hand in front of his nose, and take another step. Once in a while, bring the treat up to your chest and then down to the dog's nose again so that the dog gets used to paying attention and looking up.

Never drag your dog if he is scared to walk on leash. Just be patient and wait for him to move forward, and reward him when he does.

Repeat this exercise until your dog is a super one-step sitter. Now try taking two steps, and then stop and sit. Increase the number of steps as your dog gets the hang of it. You can soon take three steps, then four. In very little time, you'll be able to walk all over with a loose leash, and your dog will sit when you stop. If the leash gets tight at any point, do not continue walking—by doing so, you would be rewarding your dog for pulling. Instead, stop and ask him to sit. He'll quickly learn that watching you and stopping when you do is the way to keep the walk going.

Even a little dog has a lot of pull!

Occasionally, release your dog after he has sat at your side or walked nicely for a bit, and let him investigate at the end of the leash for a moment. This way, you are using the distractions in the environment as rewards for walking nicely by your side.

Dinner and a Stroll

Take your dog's dinner with you when you walk your dog. Have your dog on a long leash and let him wander a few feet away from you. Call your dog, and praise him when he looks at you. Kneel down or back up to encourage him to head toward you. Praise him when he does, and give him a piece of his food when he gets to you. In a walk around your block, you should be able to repeat this process twenty to thirty times, and you will have dramatically increased your dog's recall reliability.

Don't Use Physical Prompting in Leash Training

Numerous leash techniques are used to train dogs to stop pulling and walk calmly. When most people think of a dog walking close, they immediately think of leash and collar training—jerking the dog this way and that to get him to stay by your side. While you can train a dog to walk close by using the leash in this way, this method is extremely deceptive. Of course, when you're walking on public property or anyplace that might be dangerous, you want your dog on leash for safety's sake. But I strongly advise you not to use a leash as the only training aid. If you think about it, the very notion of having to jerk the dog around is antithetical to teaching the dog to want to be close to you.

Most important, what may start off as gentle physical prompting almost always turns into physical force. Eventually, most dogs become desensitized to leash corrections and end up pulling more vehemently. So do not rely on using the leash for corrections to get the dog to come close or keep close.

Come and Get It!

Have a friend or family member hold your dog in another room while you prepare his meal. Call your dog (tell the person to let go when you do so), and reward him for coming to find you by giving him his meal.

What If My Dog Won't Walk?

Nothing will make your dog balk and want to move away from you more than jerking the leash and dragging him. If your dog lags, be careful not to reinforce this behavior by giving him attention when he stops. Instead, stand or kneel facing away from your dog and wait. Praise your dog if he moves even one inch toward you. It doesn't matter how long it takes (it shouldn't be more than a minute or two)—eventually he will come. Then walk another few feet away and repeat if he stops.

The Tie That Binds: Umbilical Cord Training

Leaving a young or new dog to explore the house on his own is asking for trouble. Even being in the same room as your new dog may not be sufficient supervision. It takes very little time for a dog to chew a piece of furniture or soil the carpet. Occasionally tying your dog to you (around your waist) is an effective way to allow your dog to spend time with you around the home under safe and constant supervision when he is not resting in his long-term confinement area. As a bonus, within a few days, your dog will develop the habit of walking by your side around the house and settling at your side when you stop. This is a terrific foundation for walking nicely by your side on leash outside.

If your dog is afraid of leash walking, take him out for numerous confidence-building training sessions on leash. You don't want to take him with you on an errand when you may be in a hurry and get frustrated with your dog. Once you have taken the time to teach your dog to enjoy leash walking, he can come along with you on all your errands.

Hand Targeting

Hand targeting is when your dog touches the palm of your hand with his nose when you request him to do so. Hand targeting can aid you in teaching your dog to walk nicely by your side (he will learn that he has to stay close enough to touch your hand occasionally when requested), to go where you want him to (you can use your hand to direct him to his bed), and to teach many tricks (including the spin). As a wonderful side effect, hand targeting also teaches your dog to be confident and enthusiastic about hands reaching toward him.

You can also teach your dog to target other things, such as the tip of a stick or another person. Targeting is a valuable skill for dogs who perform commercial or film work (think of the dog running to a spot away from a handler and touching an object such as a doorknob), but it can also be extremely valuable for your star pet dog!

Hand targeting is valuable because:

1. It may help your dog learn to approach and interact politely with strangers (they present their hand, and your dog touches it to say hello).

2. It is a great way to help prevent and solve behavior problems, such as guarding food or other resources, since it gives you a calm, easy way to redirect your dog away from an object and to your hand.

3. It is a good tool for perfecting a reliable recall. When your dog begins to return to you after you call him, presenting your hand gives him a specific spot to head to rather than potentially circling around you and playing a game of catch-me-if-you-can.

4. It can be added to the list of behaviors your dog can use to ask nicely for things. For example, you can ask him to hand target before he gets to play in the dog run, walk out the front door, or come up on the couch for a hug.

Teaching Your Dog to Target

To teach your dog to hand target, present the palm of your hand no more than 6 inches away from your dog's nose. Your curious dog is likely to touch your palm. Mark the exact moment you feel his wet nose on your skin with a click or by saying "yes," and then offer him one tiny treat. If he doesn't touch your hand promptly, just wait. If he is on a leash that you are stepping on or have tied to a stable object, he isn't going anywhere and will eventually touch your hand out of curiosity or because there isn't much else available to him at the moment.

Why Mark?

Since the act of a dog touching his nose to your hand is an extremely brief behavior, you need a way to very accurately tell your dog that what he did at that *exact* moment is what earns him the food treat. After ten to thirty repetitions of clicking or saying "yes" at the exact moment your dog touches your hand with his nose (and rewarding him with a tiny treat for doing so), your dog will start to understand that touching your hand with his nose is what earns him a reward.

Avoid Pushing Your Hand in Your Dog's Face

It is best to avoid pushing your hand into your dog's face. The object of this exercise is to teach your dog to touch your hand, not to teach your

Teach your dog to touch his nose to the palm of your hand, and you have a great foundation for getting him to come when called and a very good way of redirecting his attention.

dog to tolerate you touching his nose! Also, be careful not to hold the treats from your other hand too close to your dog's face, at least not in the initial stages of teaching. They may be too distracting.

Moving Forward with Hand Targeting

Once your dog is touching your hand consistently and enthusiastically when it is presented no more than 6 inches away from his nose, you can start to present your hand a bit farther away or in a slightly different position. Expect your dog to be less reliable in his responses as you change the criteria of what you are asking (your hand is farther away, higher, lower, or on a different side of his head). Just stick with each new way of presenting your hand until your dog touches it reliably. Repetition and reinforcement for correct responses will strengthen this behavior, and then you can move on and ask your dog to hand target in yet another slightly different way.

Adding the Cue Word "Touch"

When you are confident that your dog understands to touch your hand when you present it (you should be confident enough to bet $100 that the behavior will happen!), say "touch" right before you present your hand. Repeating this process many times in three- to five-minute training sessions will set the groundwork for your dog to understand that the word "touch" means to find your hand and touch it with his nose.

Now, if you like, you can teach your dog to touch your hand *only* when he hears you say "touch." Present your hand without saying the word. If your dog touches it, don't reward. He may seem confused for a moment since he has been rewarded before for touching your hand whether or not you say "touch." Continue rewarding your dog for touching your hand when you say the cue and present your hand, and ignore those touches offered without you saying the cue.

Time to Reward Randomly

Your ultimate goal is to get your dog to respond properly to you without having to reward him every time. Of course, in the pet dog world, you don't have to phase out the treats, toys, or games entirely, because a lot of people like giving their dog rewards. Continued reinforcement is the best way to maintain reliable behavior. Plus, I love rewarding my dogs; it makes both of us happy. But you do want to know that your dog will comply with your requests even without the presence of food or toys in your hands.

When you can reliably get a behavior using food or toy rewards, it is time to begin using them randomly, varying these two rewards with others, such as the toss of a ball, a walk, or attention.

A dog trained with dog-friendly methods is motivated to play the training game because of the prospect of lots of great rewards (like praise, treats, and toys), but also because the game itself is fun. Part of what makes it fun is randomizing rewards. Much like a gambler who enjoys the prospect of never knowing exactly what a slot machine will produce, keeping your dog guessing by randomizing rewards will get him hooked on playing the training game with you.

1. Keep your dog guessing "what" (throw a tennis ball instead of giving a treat).

2. Keep your dog guessing "where" (rewards come from your pocket, the cupboard, or somebody else).

3. Keep your dog guessing "when" (ask for more behaviors for fewer rewards).

Shout and Treat!

Yell for your dog to come to you, and when he does, lavish him with lots of praise, toys, or kibble and a few treats. He'll learn that urgency in your voice doesn't mean that you're angry; it just means to get there fast and get hugs and treats! In an emergency situation, you will probably yell at your dog, but if you've practiced this way in non-emergency situations, your dog is much less likely to be spooked if you panic.

8

Behavior Problems

In the wild, dogs live in dens and have their own way of going about things. But if you want your dog to live in your home with you, you must teach her the human way of living. Specifically, you have to teach your dog to appropriately redirect her normal and natural behaviors. Failing to learn where to relieve herself, what to chew, when to bark, when to jump up, and where to dig are the top reasons the relationship fails and people give up their dogs. Luckily, these techniques are so simple to teach that you and your dog are all but guaranteed to have a long and happy life together.

Barking Nine to Five

What does a bark mean? Well, what does a word mean? The bark is a dog's word, and it can mean many things. Your dog barks when she's alerting you to an intruder, when she's afraid or stressed, when she's feeling playful, and when she's bored. Barking is caused by the presence of stimuli (strange people, dogs, sights, or sounds) or the owner's absence, and can be an attention-seeking mechanism.

The easiest way to control barking is to socialize your dog so that she's comfortable with lots of people, places, and things and to instill in her a strong chew-toy habit so that she is mentally and physically exercised and occupied. But, just as you would not attempt to completely silence a person, you shouldn't try to completely silence your dog. Your dog just needs to learn some basic bark control—when it is appropriate and acceptable to bark and for how long.

Regardless of the reason for your dog's barking, your goal is to properly socialize your dog, teach your dog to focus on something other than barking, and teach your dog to speak and be quiet on command so that you can control when and for how long she barks.

Most behavior problems are unintentionally encouraged during the first few weeks a puppy or dog is in her new home. For example, this puppy is learning that barking is a good way to be the center of attention.

Alarm Barker

Dogs who bark at the presence of intruders can be valuable assets. It's ironic that barking dogs are such a problem in our society, inasmuch as barking as an alarm must have been one of the main reasons we domesticated dogs in the first place. Usually, it isn't the barking that is a problem—it's just that the dog is a little too enthusiastic. Most people *want* their dogs to let them know when someone has stepped onto the property. Barking becomes a problem only if the dog doesn't settle down when you ask her to.

Until you have this problem under control, keep your dog on leash at all times when you are home to supervise her. This way, you have a gentle, effective means of preventing her from rushing to the door and barking uncontrollably.

Teach your dog to bark and be quiet on cue and thereby have an on/off switch. To do so, invite three friends to come over for a speak-and-shush party, and within 30 minutes you'll have the foundation of a well-trained barker and shusher.

Have your dog's dinner kibble on hand. Ask your dog to speak (request), instruct your visitors to knock on the door when they hear you say this (stimulus), and let your dog know that barking was the right response by saying "thank you." At this point, your dog may look a bit shocked. After all, she's probably used to being yelled at when she barks.

Now, to get her to be quiet, say "shush" (request) and waggle a very tasty treat in front of her nose. Once she sniffs the food, she'll be quiet (she can't sniff and bark at the same time), so give it to her as a reward.

Repeat this process many times, and your dog will become increasingly aware of how much fun it is to speak on request and how rewarding it is to shush on request.

Yard Barker

Barking dogs are one of the most common complaints of urban and suburban neighbors. Obviously, a dog left outside will alert to all the visual and auditory stimuli.

Dogs are usually relegated to the yard because they're not housetrained or chew-toy trained. If that's the case, housetrain and chew-toy train your dog. Rescue her from the backyard and bring her into your home!

Giving your dog a few well-stuffed chew toys is the easiest and most effective way to prevent barking. This way, she has something to think about other than barking. A well-stuffed chew toy will keep your dog busy for an hour or more (this means no time for barking). If you need to, put her food bowl away and feed her only from her chew toys. You'll keep her very busy!

No Yard Dogs, Please

It's not a great idea to leave your dog alone in your yard. Not only will her housetraining and manners deteriorate, but she's also likely to learn and engage in activities you won't appreciate, such as digging, barking, or escaping. Moreover, she's vulnerable to a number of dangers, including being stolen, poisoned, harassed by passersby, or hurt by an animal that comes into the yard.

Attention-Seeking Barker

Many people inadvertently train their dogs to bark for attention by responding to barks and whines. This is especially true with young puppies and very tiny dogs whose little whimpers and whines bring their owners running. However, regardless of size, most dogs develop a formidable bark that is likely to become more demanding in nature as they learn to expect a response. What starts off as a soft little whimper can quickly turn into an ear-piercing shout—the dog's way of saying "I want attention! And I want it now!"

You can prevent your dog from learning that barking and whining is an effective way to get your attention simply by ignoring any vocalization. Admittedly, doing so can be difficult at first, but most dogs figure out quickly that vocalizing doesn't work. They are also quick to figure out if it does work, so be careful not to reinforce this behavior occasionally by talking to or even looking at your dog when she barks for attention.

If your dog has already been reinforced for barking for attention, you can teach her that it no longer works simply by starting fresh and ignoring her when she barks. When you're relaxed and in a good mood, tie your dog to a secure spot in the house and get a good book to read. Sit next to your dog and ignore her. If she whines or barks, ignore her or move a short distance away. When she's quiet, even for a moment, move closer. Your dog will soon realize that barking means you leave and quiet means you return. When she's quiet for a few moments, you can click or say "yes" and reward her with a tiny treat. You can also praise her very calmly.

If your dog is barking for your attention . . .

. . . simply teach her that it will have the opposite effect.

Owner-Absent Barker

What if your dog barks because she's bored or stressed when left at home alone? Unfortunately, our canine friends are often left alone for long periods. Being social animals, dogs find it tough to understand why their families leave them. However, you can teach your dog to tolerate and even enjoy your absence.

Some dogs were specifically bred to be companions, and they may especially miss you when left at home alone. So teach them right away to tolerate and even enjoy time by themselves.

First, teach your dog to spend time alone while you're at home. Most people make the mistake of spending all their time at home with their dogs at their sides. While this act may seem kind and loving, it only makes matters worse. Your dog will become accustomed to constant companionship and will be more likely to fall apart when you leave.

Instead, teach your dog to enjoy quiet moments by herself while you're at home so that she'll feel more confident when you're not there. Frequently and for short periods, confine your dog to another room, in her crate, or on a tie-down and give her a couple of well-stuffed chew toys to occupy her time. In fact, make a habit of giving your dog as many of her favorite things as possible (including her meals in food-dispensing toys) when you ask her to be by herself.

Whining

It's best not to attempt to soothe your dog when she whines. Soothing usually serves only to reward and reinforce the whining behavior. Instead, ignore your dog until she's quiet. After ten to fifteen seconds of silence, let her know that you like this quiet behavior by praising her calmly and, if you like, by offering her a food reward.

Jumping Up

Dogs jump on people to say hello in an effort to be friendly, and because many dogs have not learned the requisite impulse control to manage their exuberance. Although you want your dog to be friendly with people, her excessive enthusiasm may keep friends away and make all that wonderful socialization go to waste. Your dog deserves to be taught how to greet people properly so that she can enjoy the pleasure of human company.

Frequently, dogs are reinforced for jumping up during puppyhood. It can be quite charming for a little pup to bound up to us enthusiastically and jump all about. However, reinforcing this behavior really isn't fair to the pup, since it is unlikely that the behavior will be deemed appropriate once she is a grown-up dog.

Most adult dog jumping occurs when owners come home feeling guilty for having left the dog and in some cases are actually somewhat pleased that the dog is so happy to see them. Jumping up is also frequently reinforced by people outside your family who respond to your dog out of nervousness or embarrassment or because they don't really mind the jumping since they don't have to live with it long-term. But you do!

Understandably, most people would prefer to be greeted by a dog who has been taught to sit to say hello.

Teach your dog to stand or sit to greet people and you won't have to worry about her jumping. Most important, focus on managing your dog by keeping her on leash when she greets people until she has learned how to greet politely.

You can begin using the capturing method by simply waiting for your dog to sit and ignoring everything else she does, whether it be bouncing around or barking. The moment her rear hits the ground, say "yes" or click and offer a tiny treat. Tell her "okay" (or say whichever release word you've chosen) so she knows that she can get up, and then take a step away from her so she follows you to "greet" you again.

Wait for the sit, and then mark and reward it. It shouldn't take long for her to learn that sitting is the way to get rewarded.

When she sits automatically when you stop, you're ready to progress to more difficult greetings. Take a few more steps between sits—the more you move, the more likely your dog is to get revved up. You can also try being verbally playful with her once you stop walking. Gradually increase your enthusiasm, and eventually you should be able to be as playful as you like, and your dog should respond with an equally happy, but seated, greeting.

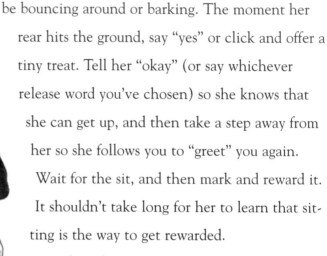

Until your dog learns good greeting manners, keep him on leash so that you can manage and prevent inappropriate encounters, such as jumping.

When you think that your dog is ready, have family members enter the front door numerous times during three- to five-minute training sessions, and then try inviting a few friends over. Have your dog's meal or special treats ready. For each person who comes to the door, simply wait for your dog to sit, and then give her one piece of her food. If each person is kind enough to leave and come back ten times, you'll have thirty practice sessions by inviting just three people over. If you want to speed things up a bit, lure your dog into a sit.

People have devised all sorts of ways to physically punish dogs for jumping up, such as jerking the leash, holding the dog's paws, stepping on the dog's hind feet, kneeing the dog in the chest, and flipping the dog over backward. Why not just train the dog to greet people appropriately? Why not train her to sit?

This dog may learn not to jump up, but she may also learn that she doesn't want to greet people at all.

When an overly enthusiastic greeting is met with a physical punishment and/or a verbal correction, the dog may be left thinking, "I just wanted to say 'hi.' Wow, they must be angry at me. Let me try and make up by greeting them happily again." Indeed, punishment often prompts your dog to jump up with renewed vigor, for which she is then met with a more severe punishment. The act of greeting people now becomes a confusing prospect. Some dogs with softer temperaments may be so confused and panicked that they begin to urinate when greeting people. What the owners perceive as a disgusting behavior is actually a way for the dog to say how submissive she feels in the face of potential punishment.

Chewing Inappropriate Items

Dogs are superbly investigative creatures who use their teeth (since they don't have hands) to hold and manipulate things. It is normal for dogs to pick up objects and carry them about and, oftentimes, to find spots to store those objects.

Puppies are especially likely to use their mouths to investigate and chew objects because they are programmed to learn as much as possible about the world in a very short period. Young puppies also go through the painful process of teething as they lose their baby teeth and adult teeth grow in their place. Chewing can help alleviate the pain of teething.

The most important strategy in preventing the chewing of inappropriate items is to provide your dog with plenty of appropriate chew toys. I recommend toys that are hollow and can be stuffed with food. Also, don't allow your dog to have too much freedom in your home before she can handle it. It is advisable to keep her on leash when you can supervise her. Avoid playing roughly or otherwise encouraging the dog to nip at hands, clothing, hair, or inappropriate objects.

Couch Hog

Many dogs learn to see soft, comfortable areas to rest (such as your couch and bed) as valuable places that they are unlikely to relinquish readily. If you choose to permit your dog to share these resting areas with you, be sure to use preventative measures in order to avoid the unpleasant situation of having a dog who won't get off when asked. In the worst-case scenario, a dog may growl, bark, or bite when asked to move. If this is the case, seek the assistance of a professional trainer immediately.

The goal is to teach your dog that when she leaves a desirable spot at your request, good things are likely to happen. Start with the dog on the floor as you sit on the couch. Encourage her up onto the couch. If she isn't big enough to jump up, you can use a pillow or two or give her dog steps to step on. To get her to jump off the couch, pat the floor and encourage your dog to jump off. Click or say "yes" when she does and give her a tiny treat. It won't take her long to realize that getting up on the couch isn't so exciting, but jumping off when you ask her to is terrific!

Separation Issues

Dogs are social creatures who don't like to be left alone. Sadly, most pet dogs spend a large part of their time by themselves. To prepare your dog to enjoy time spent at home alone, make sure that she frequently spends time by herself while you're at home. You don't want to set a precedent of constant companionship—this just sets your dog up to fall apart when you leave. Some dogs react to being left alone by indulging in their favorite pastimes. These might include being destructive to the home, barking, or marking the house with urine and feces.

Many owners have difficulty ignoring their dogs during the course of the day, especially when their dogs seek attention. Interacting with the dog almost constantly becomes a habit. Instead, try using a crate or tie-down. A *tie-down* is a leash that can't be chewed through that you attach to a stable object or an eye hook in the wall. The tie-down should be only about 3 feet long, just long enough for the dog to sit, lie down, stand up, and turn around. It is sort of like a crate without walls. Put a couple of food-stuffed toys in your dog's crate or by the tie-down to give her something to do while she spends time alone.

Garbage Raiding

Dogs are naturally investigative creatures; like many of us, they are always on the lookout for a tasty morsel. Therefore, it should come as no surprise that your dog might try to figure out a way to gain access to the garbage, which is surely full of delicious leftovers.

To discourage garbage raiding, get a garbage can that has a locking lid. Or simply put the garbage can in a place your dog can't reach, such as under the sink. If you attempt to correct your dog when you catch her raiding the can, chances are all she will learn is to avoid going on a garbage hunt when you're around. You'll essentially have created an owner-absent garbage hound.

Eating Feces

Eating feces is a distasteful habit that many dogs will engage in if given the chance. Most commonly, dogs will eat the stools of other animals. Less commonly, dogs may eat their own stools.

The most likely cause of this habit is boredom. However, some experts suggest that it may be caused by a nutritional deficiency, so make sure that your dog's diet is well balanced and speak with your dog's veterinarian to rule out this possibility.

The solution to feces eating starts with preventing your dog from having the opportunity to practice this behavior. Each time she does it, the habit becomes stronger. If you are walking in the woods with your dog, simply call her away from any stool and reward her with a treat. If you let your dog out in the yard to eliminate, go with her and clean up her stool promptly.

Some people have had success with food additives designed to make the stools distasteful. More important, be sure to provide your dog with plenty of chew toys to keep her busy.

Digging

Your dog has lots of reasons for wanting to dig. Digging is fun and relieves boredom. It also creates a cool place to lie in hot weather, and in some cases dogs dig to escape an enclosure. To prevent unwanted digging, don't let your dog spend unsupervised time in the yard. Go outside and watch her play or, better yet, play with her. If you can't supervise, bring her indoors.

Terriers dig? Of course they do! Terrier comes from the word terra, meaning earth. Terriers were born and bred to dig.

If you don't want to ban digging altogether, you can teach your dog that it isn't digging you dislike, but digging *everywhere*. Choose one spot and designate it as her digging pit. Think of it as her sandbox. Let her watch you bury a couple of tasty chew toys. Then encourage her to dig in that spot to get them out. Your dog will learn that this is the best (and only) place to dig, because it's where the buried treasure is and because you are there to help her choose the right spot.

Hyperactivity

It's all too common for dog trainers to hear owners describe their dogs as hyperactive. In fact, most of these dogs aren't really hyperactive; they just have the typical energy level of a dog (high) and are in a home where the owner has the typical energy level of a person (not quite as high as a dog, especially after a long day at work).

The simple solution to this "problem" is to make sure that your dog:

◆   Has adequate exercise. Talk to your vet about your particular dog's needs.

◆   Is fed the appropriate food. Food affects a dog's behavior, just like it does with people.

◆   Is mentally stimulated. Hide lots of fun, educational toys, such as those that can be stuffed with food, around the house.

◆   Is taught to have an on/off switch. Many times throughout the day, play with your dog and get her into an energetic mood. Interrupt the play many times by asking your dog to lie down. To begin, ask her to lie down for just a few seconds before you release her, and then gradually increase the length of time you expect her to control herself and remain lying down. Continually getting your dog excited and then settling her down turns what could be a problem (an excited, high-energy dog) into a reward for calm behavior. This is a perfect example of a life reward: using something your dog likes (high-energy play) that is not concrete (not a treat or praise) to reward her for behavior that you like (lying down calmly).

Chasing

Chasing other animals and objects is a great thrill for many dogs, especially sight hounds and herding breeds. These dogs were bred specifically to chase and are likely to be highly stimulated by cars, bicycles, moving animals, and joggers. Chasing is basically an extension of the dog's prey drive. Although this behavior is normal and natural, it can lead to trouble in many ways. A dog who chases can become a neighborhood nuisance and, worse, can cause serious injury to herself, another animal, or a person. If your dog has a habit of chasing, keep her on leash at all times when outdoors until you are confident that you have resolved the issue.

One of the most important aspects of preventing and resolving chasing issues is to teach your dog to come reliably when called (see page 174) and to hand target for attention (see page 191). When appropriate, it is also important to set up practice sessions with whatever is stimulating your dog to chase. For example, if your dog chases people riding bicycles, invite a friend over to work on conditioning your dog to remain calm and under your control when your friend passes by on the bike.

Plan three- to five-minute sessions at times when your dog is hungry so that you have the best chance of attracting and keeping her focus, and be sure to keep her on leash. Always start at a distance far greater than what you think your dog can handle. Perhaps you need to have your friend pass by at twenty feet away in order for your dog to be able to focus on you.

Practice hand targeting, sit, down, stand, and any other skills you have taught your dog as a way of instructing her to focus on you and respond reliably to your requests. It is important to confirm that your dog responds reliably to requests in a stationary position before you can expect her to respond to you (and come back when called) when moving away from you at a distance.

Gradually decrease the distance between your dog and the bicycle (or whatever stimulus you are working with) when you feel that your dog can handle it. Because this closer range will be more challenging for your dog, be sure to increase the value and frequency of the rewards you give her.

Fear of People

Reward-based techniques are the method of choice when dealing with fearful dogs. If you have a dog who's a little afraid of or doesn't like people, you need to find a way to get this message across to the dog: "Hey, buddy, I like you. If you'll just come close, I'll give you a bit of food or a toy." Using food as a lure is an effective way to communicate when the dog is afraid of your voice or physical contact (in which case you cannot praise or pat), and it's easy to toss a piece of food to the ground close by. Eventually, the dog will come closer, lured by the food first on the ground and then in your hand.

Make sure that your dog is extremely interested in food by starting this exercise well before mealtimes or as a substitute for them. Sit in an armchair and scatter food around you (or a friend). Your dog can approach and retreat as she likes. As she comes closer, she gets the food, and as she runs off, she gets nothing. Once she is more interested in the food (this may take some time depending on how fearful your dog is with a particular person, so it's best to focus on proximity first), you can take the food and talk gently to the dog in the language she has learned: come, sit, and down. This in itself is like a behavioral pacifier and will accelerate the bonding process. That is, if your dog is confident in her understanding of what is expected when asked to sit or lie down, her overall confidence may improve. This clarity means that it is easier for the dog to remain calm and focused on what to do to get a treat.

A Tiny Touch Can Lead to So Much!

Teaching your dog to hand target is an invaluable aid in resolving fear issues. The more she is rewarded for touching her nose to the hand of a variety of people, the more her confidence in and enthusiasm for people will improve.

If you think your dog is fearful, stressed, or worried, for your dog's sake please work on this problem before it worsens. Being anxious is no fun. If your dog has any kind of aggression problem, seek help from a professional trainer immediately (call 800-PET-DOGS or go to www.apdt.com).

Don't Be an Overprotective Owner!

Avoid being overly protective of your puppy or dog, especially if you have a little dog. More often than not, overprotectiveness creates or exacerbates fear and aggression problems.

Canine Squabbles

If your dog is unfriendly with lots of other dogs, it means that she is not adequately socialized to dogs. (But don't expect your dog to be best friends with every dog; after all, we aren't friends with every person!) A well-socialized dog may still have occasional arguments. However, socialization ensures that your dog has the requisite social savvy to enjoyably and confidently interact with unfamiliar dogs she may meet and to resolve arguments with other dogs without doing damage. It is easiest to socialize your dog when she is young, but it is never too late to make her more dog friendly. If possible and appropriate, find dog social groups in your area where you can plan play dates with suitable dogs.

Hand Targeting to the Rescue Yet Again!

If you notice your dog focusing on and becoming tense at a passing dog, you can practice redirecting her attention and rewarding her for focusing on something positive by asking her to hand target. Position your hand so that your dog has to turn away from the other dog (who is a safe distance away, of course), and mark and reward for a prompt response in such a distracting environment.

A lack of proper socialization means that your dog will never get to fully enjoy fun and games with other dogs.

Don't Make Matters Worse

Owners often inadvertently train dog-to-dog aggression. When an owner sees another dog and tightens the leash, the owner's tension is often relayed to the dog. The dog growls, and the owner tightens the leash more and maybe yells at the dog to "be nice!" Over time, the dog becomes conditioned to tense up as she makes the association between other dogs approaching and her owner's anxiety. So now the dog wants the other dog to stay away, and one of the ways she tries to accomplish this is by growling and barking.

Furthermore, if your dog is uncomfortable with another dog, tightening the leash excludes flight from her possible options and leaves her with fight as the primary option. Tightening the leash also distorts your dog's body language and all but forces her to lean forward—a posture that the other dog may perceive as threatening.

Obviously, you must keep your dog on leash for safety, but you've got to learn to control her without tightening the leash. By keeping the leash loose and remaining calm, you may convince your dog to do the same! Also consider using a head halter (see Chapter 2)—this is a time when a head halter can be very handy.

When your dog is under-socialized, everyday encounters can be extremely stressful.

Don't punish your dog for barking or growling at other dogs. The punishment may teach your dog to think, "I don't like being around other dogs because I am punished whenever they show up, so I'll bark to keep them away." Instead, try to focus on making your dog enjoy the presence of other dogs by associating them with things she likes.

Use Reward Training

For dog-to-dog issues, the method of choice is capturing, and the best feedback is high-value treats and praise. Start by exposing your dog to one friendly dog at a time, at a safe distance that seems comfortable for your dog. If she lunges or barks, then you are too close. Whenever your dog does *anything* you deem appropriate around this other dog, mark and reward the behavior immediately. This includes looking at you, standing, sitting, or lying down calmly. It is important to keep a careful eye on your dog and be ready to give immediate feedback for even a moment of

Nothing makes a dog more reactive than a tight leash, and screaming at her will only make things worse.

appropriate behavior. As always, repetitive reinforcement will increase the likelihood, frequency, and duration of these behaviors.

Use the "Jolly" Training Routine

To begin this routine, go outside and sit on a park bench. Whenever you see another dog, say, "Oh, look, here comes a cookie dog." As soon as your dog sees the other dog, give her a treat. Even if your dog is tense and growling, and one might say that you are rewarding the dog for growling and acting badly around other dogs, things will improve quickly. The dog can't help but make a positive association between the other dog and the high-value treat, and soon she will look forward to other dogs approaching.

Be sure to give your dog enough space from the other dog to feel safe and comfortable. And watch for early signs of discomfort, such as yawning and excessive panting. You don't want to push your dog too far too fast.

A variation of this game is to get very happy whenever another dog passes by. Your dog can't fail to make the association between the appearance of another dog and your positive change in mood. This is important because your (negative) change in mood may have partially caused the problem in the first place or made the problem worse. If the dogs were left to their own devices, they would probably resolve the problem amicably.

In some cases, it helps to hand-feed your dog and get her fixated on an object (like a chew toy or a white sterilized bone). It will give her something to focus on and associate the presence of dogs with things she likes.

By rewarding your dog in the presence of other dogs, your dog will soon begin to associate the presence of other dogs with rewards.

Every Big Journey
Starts with a Tiny Step

If your dog is afraid of people or other dogs, it may take a bit of time for her to regain confidence. These situations require as much compassion and patience as dealing with human fears and phobias.

Resource Guide

Association of Pet Dog Trainers

This group is the *best* source for finding a trainer in your area and for information about dog-training seminars.

Association of Pet Dog Trainers
150 Executive Center Dr., Box 35
Greenville, SC 29615
800-PET-DOGS
Fax: 864-331-0767
www.apdt.com

Books

Arden, Andrea. *Train Your Dog the Lazy Way*. New York: Alpha Books, 1998.

Donaldson, Jean. *The Culture Clash*. Oakland, CA: James & Kenneth Publishers, 1996.

Dunbar, Ian, PhD, MRCVS. *Doctor Dunbar's Good Little Dog Book*. Oakland, CA: James & Kenneth Publishers, 2003.

Need more help building your perfect dog?

Dunbar, Ian, PhD, MRCVS. *How to Teach a New Dog Old Tricks*. Oakland, CA: James & Kenneth Publishers, 1998.

Pryor, Karen. *Don't Shoot the Dog!: The New Art of Teaching and Training*. New York: Bantam Books, 1999.

Videos

Broitman, Virginia, and Sherri Lippman. *Take a Bow . . . Wow! Easy Tricks Any Dog Can Do*. Doswell, VA: Take a Bow Wow, 1995.

Dunbar, Ian, PhD, MRCVS. *Dog Training for Children*. Oakland, CA: James & Kenneth Publishers, 1996.

Dunbar, Ian, PhD, MRCVS. *Sirius Puppy Training*. Oakland, CA: James & Kenneth Publishers, 1987.

Dunbar, Ian, PhD, MRCVS. *Training the Companion Dog*. (Set of four videos, "Socialization," "Behavior Problems," "Leash Walking and Jumping Up," and "Recalls and Stays.") Oakland, CA: James & Kenneth Publishers, 1992.

Dunbar, Ian, PhD, MRCVS. *Training Dogs with Dunbar: Fun Training for You and Your Dog*. Oakland, CA: James & Kenneth Publishers, 1996.

Hunthausen, Wayne. *Dogs, Cats & Kids*. Donald Manelli & Associates, Inc., 1996.

Pryor, Karen. *Puppy Love: Raise Your Dog the Clicker Way*. Sunshine Books, 1999.

Catalogs

General Pet Supplies

Cherry Brook
Rte. 57, P.O. Box 15
Broadway, NJ 08808
800-524-0820
908-689-7979
www.cherrybrook.com

Doctors Foster and Smith
2253 Air Park Rd.
P.O. Box 100
Rhinelander, WI 54501
800-381-7179
www.drsfostersmith.com

J-B Wholesale Pet Supplies, Inc.
5 Raritan Rd.
Oakland, NJ 07436
800-526-0388
www.jbpet.com

Pet Books (Including Rare and Hard-to-Find Titles)

Dogwise, Direct Book Service's Dog & Cat Book Catalogue
701 B Poplar
Wenatchee, WA 98801
800-776-2665
509-663-9115
www.dogwise.com

More Fun and Games

Agility

Agility is one of the modern dog games that has its roots in friendly train-ing. It requires off-leash control and an enthusiastic spirit on the part of both dog and owner. For more information, contact:

Agility Association of Canada (AAC)
638 Wonderland Rd., S.
London, Ontario
Canada N6K 1L8
519-473-3410
www.aac.ca

Don't let the term Non-Sporting Group deceive you; all of these dogs were bred for special functions, and some of them are quite sporty! They enjoy as much mental and physical exercise as any dog.

North American Dog Agility Council (NADAC)
P.O. Box 1206
Colbert, OK 74733
208-689-3803
www.nadac.com

United States Dog Agility Association (USDAA)
P.O. Box 850955
Richardson, TX 75085
972-487-2200
Fax: 972-272-4404
www.usdaa.com

Canine Good Citizen (CGC) Program

The Canine Good Citizen Program is a test developed by the American Kennel Club. It is used to evaluate a dog's basic manners and includes exercises such as greeting a friendly stranger, sitting politely for petting, walking through a crowd, coming when called, and supervised separation. Contact the American Kennel Club for more information.

Flyball

Flyball is a fast-paced sport that requires your dog to race to a box that holds a tennis ball, press a lever to release the ball, catch it, and race back to you. It is wild and crazy fun! To learn more, contact:

North American Flyball Association (NAFA)
1400 W. Devon Ave., #512
Chicago, IL 60660
800-318-6312
www.flyball.org

Kennel Clubs and Registries

American Kennel Club (AKC)

The AKC is a registry for purebred dogs and also sponsors the Canine Good Citizen test, agility competitions, Earthdog Tests, Lure Coursing, Tracking, Herding, Field Trials and Hunting Tests, Conformation shows, and Obedience Trials.

American Kennel Club
5580 Centerview Dr.
Raleigh, NC 27606
919-233-9767
Fax: 919-233-3627
www.akc.org

American Mixed Breed Owner Registry (AMBOR)

American Mixed Breed Owner Registry
P.O. Box 36
Springfield, WI 53716
www.amborusa.com

Canadian Kennel Club (CKC)

The CKC is a registry for purebred dogs and sponsors Agility, Hunting, Terrier, and Obedience Trials.

Canadian Kennel Club
89 Skyway Ave., Suite 100
Etobicoke, Ontario
M9W 6R4
416-675-5511
www.ckc.ca

United Kennel Club (UKC)

The UKC is a registry for purebred dogs and sponsors Agility, Hunting, Terrier, and Obedience Trials.

United Kennel Club
100 E. Kilgore Rd.
Kalamazoo, MI 49002
269-343-9020
Fax: 269-343-7037
www.ukcdogs.com

Getting in Touch with the Author

For information about Andrea Arden's seminars and training classes, contact:

Andrea Arden Dog Training
212-414-9597
www.AndreaArden.com

Index